WINNING AMERICAN MAH JONGG STRATEGIES

A GUIDE FOR THE NOVICE PLAYER

ELAINE SANDBERG

Best-selling author of *A Beginner's Guide to American Mah Jongg*

TUTTLE Publishing

Tokyo | Rutland, Vermont | Singapore

Published by Tuttle Publishing, an imprint of Periplus Editions (HK) Ltd.

www.tuttlepublishing.com

Copyright © 2012 Elaine Sandberg

Library of Congress Cataloging-in-Publication Data
Sandberg, Elaine.
 Winning American Mah Jongg Strategies: A Guide for the Novice Player / by Elaine Sandberg.
    96 p. : col. ill. ; 21 cm.
 ISBN 978-0-8048-4234-1 (pbk.)
 1. Mah jong--United States. I. Title.
 GV1299.M3.S258 2012
 795.34--dc23

2011027423

ISBN 978-0-8048-4234-1

First edition
26 25 24   12 11 10   2402VP

Printed in Malaysia

Distributed by

North America, Latin America & Europe
Tuttle Publishing
364 Innovation Drive
North Clarendon,
VT 05759-9436 U.S.A.
Tel: 1 (802) 773-8930
Fax: 1 (802) 773-6993
info@tuttlepublishing.com
www.tuttlepublishing.com

Japan
Tuttle Publishing
Yaekari Building, 3rd Floor
5-4-12 Osaki Shinagawa-ku
Tokyo 141 0032
Tel: (81) 3 5437-0171
Fax: (81) 3 5437-0755
sales@tuttle.co.jp
www.tuttle.co.jp

Asia Pacific
Berkeley Books Pte. Ltd.
3 Kallang Sector, #04-01
Singapore 349278
Tel: (65) 6741-2178
Fax: (65) 6741-2179
inquiries@periplus.com.sg
www.tuttlepublishing.com

"Books to Span the East and West"

Tuttle Publishing was founded in 1832 in the small New England town of Rutland, Vermont [USA]. Our core values remain as strong today as they were then—to publish best-in-class books which bring people together one page at a time. In 1948, we established a publishing outpost in Japan—and Tuttle is now a leader in publishing English-language books about the arts, languages and cultures of Asia. The world has become a much smaller place today and Asia's economic and cultural influence has grown. Yet the need for meaningful dialogue and information about this diverse region has never been greater. Over the past seven decades, Tuttle has published thousands of books on subjects ranging from martial arts and paper crafts to language learning and literature—and our talented authors, illustrators, designers and photographers have won many prestigious awards. We welcome you to explore the wealth of information available on Asia **www.tuttlepublishing.com**.

Contents

About This Book

Today is "Mahj" day with your buddies. Greetings exchanged, the latest events shared, the "Oohs" and "Aahs" over the snacks, and finally, everyone settles in to have a fun time. The tiles are mixed, the Wall is built and quiet descends. You put your tiles up on your rack, expectations soaring. After looking them over, deflated, lament, "I don't have anything!"

I've heard this same complaint over and over in my classes and I am chagrined because 99% of the time, you do have "something" and it's possible to "Make lemonade out of lemons." If you know how.

Most novice players know the basics of the game and have at least a fairly good knowledge of the hands on the card, but their experience is limited. They have been playing for several months or a year or so and find they don't seem to win very often. They assign their lack of winning to bad luck, or a lack of Jokers, or "strategic" knowledge.

Yes, luck does play a part, as well as the help Jokers afford. But regrettably, in many instances, their Mah Jongg education did not provide them with the important strategic nuances of the game. They are left to figure those things out for themselves. These novice players are not exactly beginners, but not exactly "experienced."

My "Mah Jongg 101 B" classes are filled with these players. And in all of these classes, the same questions come up again and again. The most frequent and almost universal is the one about "finding a hand." Another is about choosing between hands and another is about changing the hand. And there are many more.

It became obvious there was a need to fulfill the request for answers from these players and it was the compelling motive for me to write this book.

In the following chapters, you will learn to interpret the information presented by these challenges, and to then choose from the strategic options available to overcome these challenges. Hopefully, you will sharpen your skills and claim "Mah Jongg!" more often.

There are Summaries and Practice exercises at the end of Chapters I and II. They are designed to help you gain confidence in your choices. At the end of the book, a quiz poses questions and situations that you confront in every game. Answer them, applying the ideas discussed in the book which, I hope, will be of value when you play in real situations.

The quiz appears on Page 69. My answers appear on Page 72 (try not to peek). Have Fun!

Sharpen Your Skills

American Mah Jongg, like all great games, is a game of challenges, strategic skill, and a little luck. It's your ability to overcome these challenges that generates the excitement of a win or the chagrin of a loss. Although there's not much you can do about luck, there's a lot you can do with what you've got to improve your strategic skills to overcome the challenges presented to you.

There is no doubt that the strategic component of the game is vital. It can determine whether you win or lose and is often the critical factor in reaching the other goal of Mah Jongg, which is to keep your opponents from winning.

But it is not a separate entity from the rest of the game.

My philosophy is that **everything** you do is a "Strategy," from the selection of your potential hand to the final discard. Decisions you make at the beginning of the game can and often do influence decisions you make at the end of the game and frequently determine its outcome. So sharpening your decision-making skills will lead you to sharpen your strategic skills.

Seasoned Mah Jongg players who have been enjoying the game for years are considered by many to be "great players." Why? Because they make their decisions quickly, with confidence, and their resulting wins generally exceed their losses. Newer players hold them in reverence for their experience and expertise. Phenomena of skill, speed, and guile, these players seem to possess certain "secrets to success." Many players who have been taught by their friends or family or have taken classes from an instructor soon realize there are serious gaps in their play, much to their dismay. Although they have been schooled in the rules and mechanics of the game, they, unfortunately, have not been introduced to these "secrets"—the necessary strategic elements and nuances essential to win.

Fortunately, there really are no secrets. There are approaches to the challenges of the game and strategies to address them, available to everyone. In the succeeding chapters we will thoroughly discuss "everything," introduce and explain specific techniques, simply and clearly, that mirror typical situations you meet in every game you play. It will improve your winning ratio and speed you on your way to joining the ranks of "great players."

Let's get to it!

Decisions, Decisions!

FIND A HAND

By the title of this chapter, you can see that the game begins largely with judgments and choices. These first choices will frequently determine the outcome of the game. Since winning is, of course, the primary objective in Mah Jongg, this chapter will help to show you how to make good first decisions that can lead to more wins.

So let's begin at the beginning—with what is the first information you use to make a decision: seeing what the 13 or 14 tiles, picked from the Wall and placed on the rack, reveal. Here you are, confronted with a conglomeration of tiles and now faced with the first of a myriad of decisions: choosing a possible hand to play.

Almost universally, the majority of beginners' and novice players' biggest complaint is that selecting a potential hand is the most difficult part of the game. Frequently heard is "I have nothing!" Or you find the tiles are potentially useful in several hands. I can sympathize with that position, because choosing at least one hand from the 50 or more possibilities available on the card can be daunting, to say nothing of frustrating.

Whatever the situation, coming to a definite decision on a hand is not always easy, nor a good idea, because the coming Charleston will offer new tiles that may strengthen your choice, give you other options, or lead to a new hand. Nor is there a lot of time to make a decision. At this point, the initial dilemma is to find a possible hand to play—fast.

So, as a novice player, is it possible to find potential hands quickly and easily? Unequivocally, yes! And here is a relatively simple approach to this task that works.

The primary idea behind selecting a hand seems at first, counter-intuitive. It is, *do not immediately look for a hand*, but find the best Section of the card that your tiles mirror because it's the Section that will lead you to find a hand.

What is a Section? The card is divided into nine or ten categories I call "Sections." Four of these are 2468(even), 13579(odd), 369, and Consecutive Run and these are the ones into which your tiles most frequently will fit. So these are the ones to which we will, primarily, turn our attention. But remember, there are nine or ten Sections on the card. So if any of these four don't produce the desired result, look to the others.

To begin with, the first thing to do when you put your tiles up on the rack is to organize them into the Sections discussed above. For example, start with putting all the even tiles together on one part of the rack, all the odd tiles together like this:

F 222 6 8, J, 1, 33 5, 9, E

Notice I've organized the tiles to look like the hands: by Section and with the Suits *and* numbers, going "up"—not just by numbers alone—the same way the Sections' hands are arranged on the card. You will never find a hand on the card that has just numbers together. It's always numbers and their Suits and/or Dragons together. Your task is to arrange the tiles to mirror at least one hand on the card. So organizing your tiles the same way the hands are organized is logical.

Keep rearranging the tiles from one Section to another. A Section should contain a minimum of five or six tiles. Three or four are weak. This arrangement allows you to plainly see what the strongest and most potent Sections are to pursue for a hand. If the tiles are predominately odd, the logical place to look for a hand is in the 13579 Section. If there are lots of 3s,6s,9s, focus your attention in the 369 Section, and so on. And sometimes there is more than one Section into which your tiles fit.

At this point, all you need to choose is a Section, not a specific hand.

POWER TILES

Once you organize the tiles into Sections, look for the Power tiles.

What are Power tiles? The combinations of Pairs, Pungs, Kongs, etc. of any tiles, including Flowers and, yes, Jokers. Power tiles are the first and most important element upon which to focus to find a Section/hand. These Power combinations are the strength of your potential hand and should be the foundation, the nucleus around which you build the hand.

Look in the Section(s) that can use them.

For example, 2s can usually be found in two different Sections, even and Consecutive Run. 9s are most often used in three different Sections, odd, 369 and again in Consecutive Run. 1s are used in the odd and Consecutive Run Sections, etc.

Look for tiles that are related to the Power by number and/or Suit and/or Dragon or Flower to enhance the Section (or hand, if you have chosen one). For example, if the Power of your hand is a Pair of 5Crak, look for other odd numbers and/or consecutive numbers as potential "relatives."

But Power tiles are only "powerful" if there is a hand on the card that can utilize them.

Example: On the 2010 card, Pairs of **2Bams** and **9Bams**, even though they're the same Suit, are not connected to each other, because there is no hand that uses these two Pairs together. Only one of the Pairs will have "Power." But a Pair of **2Bams** and a Pair of **4Craks** are connected, because there are hands in the even and Consecutive Run Sections that require 2s and 4s together, in either different or the same Suit. Both Pairs are Powerful.

Always choose the hand that uses as many Power tiles as possible. The more Power, the stronger the hand is.

Let's look at some examples to reflect the ideas outlined above. Notice I included the Flower and Joker when I counted the number of tiles in each Section.

All the examples below will reflect hands on the 2010 National Mah Jongg League card. But it doesn't matter what year your card represents. These ideas apply to any year's card.

Let's go back to the example tiles above.

F 222 6 8, J 1, 33 5, 9, E

The tiles are separated by Sections.

F 222 6 8 J	7	even
F 1, 33 5, 9 J	7	odd
F 1, 222, 33 J	8	Consecutive Run
F 33, 6 9 J	6	369

The Power of the hand is a **Pung of 2s** and **Pair of 3s**, plus a powerful and versatile Joker. 2s and 3s are consecutive odd and even numbers and **mirror the Consecutive Run Section**. So that is logically, where my search for a hand will begin. It not only is it the strongest Section but potentially utilizes all the Power tiles. And hopefully, I will find a hand that also requires Flowers.

The search in the Consecutive Run Section reveals that the 5th hand requires two Flowers and Any 3 Consecutive Numbers in three different Suits.

Here is the hand on the card.

FF 1111 **2222 3333** 5th hand

Here are my tiles.

F 1J(1) **222 33** 8 tiles

The tiles fit that description and I construct my hand utilizing the Flower, the 1 Bam, and using the Joker for another 1 Bam. And, most importantly, the hand **uses all the Power**. Eight tiles toward a Mah Jongg hand is a strong beginning.

Just to make sure the selection is the best one, let's look at the other Sections that use the Power: the even, odd and 369.

There are two possible even Section hands that use the power Pung of 2s, plus the Flower, plus 6 and 8 Dot: the 3rd and the 8th.

Here are the even hands on the card.

FF 2222 8888 DDDD   3rd hand

FF 222 444 666 88   8th hand

Here are my tiles.

F 222 8 J(D)   3rd hand 6 tiles
F 222 6 8J(8)   8th hand 7 tiles

The odd Section reveals two hands that use the Pair of **3 Crak** and the **Flower**, the 3rd and 5th. Here are the odd hands on the card.

FF 11 33 55 111 111   (Kong 1,3, or 5) 3rd hand
FFFF 1111 33 5555   5th hand

Here are my tiles.

F 33 5, 1J(1)   3rd hand   6 tiles
F J(1) 33 5   5th hand   5 tiles

Again, the 369 Section uses the Pair of **3Crak** and one hand also requires **Flowers**. Here are the 369 hands on the card.

FF 3333, 6666, 9999   3rd hand
333 6666, 666 9999   2nd hand

Here are my tiles.

> **F 33, J(6), 9**   5 tiles
> **33 J(6), 6 9**   5 tiles

All of these Sections' hands use only one Power combination and have fewer tiles toward Mah Jongg than the Consecutive Run hand. Since the 5th hand of the Consecutive Run Section is the longest and uses all the Power, my choice must be that hand.

Sometimes, at first glance **the tiles reveal seemingly disparate odd and even-numbered Power Pairs**. For example, Pairs of **4Bams** and **7Craks** seem to be unrelated. Closer examination reveals the 2nd hand in the Consecutive Run Section can use these seemingly unrelated Power Pairs.

Here is the consecutive hand on the card.

> **111 2222 333 4444**   2nd hand

I can start to build my hand using the numbers

> **444 5555, 666 7777**, utilizing both Power Pairs.

Many times your tiles will contain one Power combination with little else. Go to the Section that uses the Power.

Example: Here are 13 randomly chosen tiles.

F 1 44 9, 3 7 9, 2 5 8, D W

The Power is the **Pair of 4Dots**.

Here are the Sections that can use 4s.

F 2 8, **44**   5 Even

F 1 **44**, 2 5, 3   7 Consecutive Run

The Consecutive Run Section is the longest. The **4Dots** can be used in the 5th hand, which also utilizes the **Flower**.

Here is the hand on the card.

FF 1111 **2222 3333**   5th hand.

Here are my tiles.

F 2, **3, 44,** 5 tiles or

F **3, 44,** 5 5 tiles

Here is the 1st hand in the even Section.

FF 2222 44 66 8888

Here are my tiles:

F 2 44 8   5 tiles

Even though all hands have an average number of five tiles to start, I prefer the consecutive hands because the hands have no "gaps"—tiles required by the hand that I already have to start each combination. There is another important reason: I chose the consecutive hands because they require one Pair vs. two Pairs required in the even hand. Usually, **choose the hand that requires no Pairs vs. the hand that requires one or more Pairs**. Or choose the hand that requires the fewest number of Pairs. There will be further discussion about this later on in subsequent chapters.

Many times the hand has no Power.

Here is a common example: your tiles look like this.

F 2 7, 3 4 8, J, 1 4 5, W E D

The Sections look like this:

F 1 5, 3, 7 J	6 odd
F 2, 4 8, 4 J	6 even
F 1 4 5 D, 2, 3 4 J	9 Consecutive Run

What to do? The hand looks pretty dismal. Yes, the Consecutive Section has eight consecutive numbers and a Red Dragon. But no Section looks like a "winner," even though there are potential hands in each. Some of the hands use four tiles (weak opening hands), some use the Flower, some do not. At this point, no Section or hand is compelling. **So wait for the Charleston.** If and when you get a tile that gives you a Pair, go to the Section(s) that can utilize it and start to build your hand around it, being sure you include the Joker. If you can, choose a hand that also requires Flowers.

There are other situations that pose other problems.

Sometimes, as a sign of your Goodness, you are fortunate enough to find yourself with **three or more Jokers**. Look in the Quint Section, because you must have at least two Jokers for any of the hands. But having several Jokers at the beginning, doesn't assure a win at the end. You still have to put the Jokers to their best use. We'll discuss this idea later on in the *Let the Game Begin* Chapter.

There will be situations in which you may have **several disparate Power combinations**, for example, three Pairs—**2Dots**, **6Bams**, and **9Craks**. Some can be used for one hand and some for another. Keep them around until you're sure which you cannot use as you do the Charleston, or until the game has begun and you have made a firm decision about which hand to play. So if some Power tiles are not useful for the hand you choose, they "lose their Power." Have no regrets about getting rid of them.

There is another factor you need to consider when you approach selecting your Mah Jongg hand. It pertains to the odd Section and I call it "**High vs. Low.**"

The odd Section is usually divided into hands that require the numbers 1s, 3s, and 5s and 5s, 7s, and 9s.

So when the odd numbered tiles are predominately low, 1s, 3s, 5s, look at the 135 hands and when they are predominately high, 5s, 7s, 9s, look at the 579 hands, cutting down the search and decision time.

Now let's talk about the versatile and powerful Joker.

Jokers can *create* a hand or strengthen it.

When you arrange your tiles into Sections and hands, please include Jokers. Do not leave them out and at the end of the rack with tiles you are sure you don't want. They are an essential, crucial, and powerful part of the hand. Let's look at an example.

Here is another typical hand randomly picked from the Wall.

F 1 4 66 7, JJ, 3 5, 2 9, D

The Power is the **Pair of 6Dots** and the **two Jokers**. 6s can be used in the Consecutive Run, even, and 369 Sections. Jokers anywhere.

Here are the Sections.

F 2, 4 66 JJ	7 even tiles
F 3, 66 9 JJ	7 369 tiles
F 1 4 66 7 JJ D 2 5,3	12 consecutive tiles

The Consecutive Run Section has 12 tiles, so I will focus on the Pair of 6Dots and build the consecutive hand around the number 6 and the Pair of Jokers. In the Consecutive Run Section, the 4th hand uses the Pair of 6Dots and a closely related 7Dot, plus the Soap Dragon, plus the Flower.

Here is the hand on the card.

FFFF 1111 2222 DD

Here are my tiles.

FJ(F) 66 7J(7) D   7 tiles

Using the Jokers, I have a strong beginning hand—seven tiles to start the Charleston.

The Jokers can also help create a hand, as we see in the 2nd hand of the Consecutive Run Section, again using the Power Pair of 6Dots and the Jokers.

Here is the hand on the card.

111 2222 333 4444

Here are my tiles.

66 7, JJ(88)9   6 tiles
JJ(44)5, 66 7   6 tiles

The Jokers have become either **8Bams** or **4Bams**. Six tiles are a good opening hand to have before the Charleston begins.

There is still another Consecutive Run hand Jokers can help create, the 5th.

Here is the hand on the card.

FF 1111 2222 3333

Here are my tiles.

F 5 66 JJ(77)   6 tiles
F JJ(44) 5 66   6 tiles

Here, the Jokers become **7Bams** or **4Bams**.
The 369 Section also reveals the 3rd hand as another strong possibility.

Here is the hand on the card.

FF 3333 6666 9999

Here are my tiles.

F 3J(3), 66 9J(9)   7 tiles

Finally, let's look at the even Section, again using the Power Pairs of **6Dots** and the **Jokers**. The first hand also uses the **Flower**.

Here is the hand on the card.

FF 2222 44 66 8888   1st hand.

Here are my tiles.

F 2 4 66 JJ(88)   7 tiles

In this hand, the Jokers can provide me with **8Bams**.

In these examples, you can see how Jokers can both strengthen and create opening, viable options. The power the Jokers have is clear. And why you must include Jokers when you count and pursue a hand.

Let's summarize the ideas we've discussed so far.

SUMMARY

- Arrange your tiles according to Sections, with Suits **and** numbers going up the scale, so the arrangement of the tiles on the rack reflect the arrangement of the Sections/hands on the card.

- Look for the longest and strongest Section for hands to start the Charleston. Five or six tiles in a Section are a reasonable start. Be sure to include Flowers and Jokers when you count.

- All you need to start the Charleston is a Section. You do not need a specific hand.

- Look for the Power—combinations of any tiles, including **Jokers** and/or **Flowers**.

❀ Look in the Sections that use the Power.

❀ Look for other tiles that are related to the Power by number and/or Suit, and/or **Dragon** or **Flower** to strengthen the hand.

❀ Choose the hand that uses as many Power tiles as possible.

❀ Odd and even numbered tiles usually fit in the Consecutive Run Section.

❀ When two hands are equally strong, prefer the hand that has no gaps—tiles required by the hand you already have to start each combination.

❀ Prefer the hand that requires no Pairs or the hand that requires the least number of Pairs.

❀ The odd Section's hands are usually divided into low numbers (1s, 3s, 5s) and high numbers (5s, 7s, 9s). Select your odd hand using this guide, when appropriate.

❀ Keep disparate Pairs handy until you are sure you cannot use them, either during the Charleston or as the game begins.

❀ When you have no Power, *all you need to start the Charleston is a Section*. Wait for the Charleston to provide you with a Pair. Then look in the Sections that uses it to start a hand.

❀ Use Jokers to connect disparate Power. Use Jokers to strengthen a hand or to create a hand.

In April, every year a new card is published and it is great fun to see what surprises the card holds as each card has its distinctive "characteristics."

For example, in my study of the 2010 card I found that hands required only Pairs and Kongs of Flowers. There were no hands that required Pungs. The 13579 Section had no hands that required any Dragons. And this Section had fifty percent of the hands that required four or more Pairs. And looking for combinations of specific numbers, I found, for example, the 4th 13579 hand could use a Pung of 9s, but did not require it. A Pung of 9s could also be used in the 2nd Like Numbers hand. The other three hands in which a Pung of 9s was used were all Concealed. And to my surprise the only hand in the 2468 Section that required a Pung of eights was Concealed.

I am suggesting you study your current card to determine what are its particular characteristics that can help direct your search for a hand. The more quickly you can spot the particular anomalies of your card, the sharper your decision-making skills at selecting your hand will become. There is another big advantage to "studying the card." We will be discussing this aspect in the next chapter.

Note: Interestingly, each new card has several hands carried over from preceding year's card. There is usually a couple in each Section. Sometimes the hands are exactly the same and sometimes there's a slight variation. For example, the Pungs and Kongs exchange places or a Pair and Pung change Suits, etc. But basically, many of the same hands show up in subsequent years. Once you learn the hands for one year, it's a much simpler and easier task to become familiar with the hands of a new card. So take heart!

Selecting your hand from the 50 or more available on the card is the first of many decisions you will face, but if you follow the suggestions and the ideas we've discussed, this process loses its angst and the logic becomes evident. To help give you more confidence when choosing a tentative Section or hand, do the Practice exercise on the next page.

PRACTICE

Do the following to practice the ideas we've discussed.

With the tiles of your set turned face down and mixed, randomly select 13 tiles, place them up on your rack and follow the steps outlined in this Chapter.

Here's a tip: As you start putting your tiles up onto your rack, as soon as you spot a Pair, start thinking about the Sections in which it can be used. And look for other tiles that are connected to it. It can cut down the time it takes to make a decision about a Section and hand before the start of the Charleston.

Now, on to the next set of "Strategies"—the "You never know what you'll get," surprising Charleston.

✣ CHAPTER II ✣

The Charleston And More Decisions!

An anomaly of the Mah Jongg world, the Charleston is a procedure found only in the American variant. Its origin is unknown and its name is, perhaps, an allusion to the dance craze of the 1920s, when Mah Jongg was also a craze of the era. Or perhaps it originated in a place called Charleston. No one really knows. It was already a part of the game when the National Mah Jongg League standardized the game's rules and procedures in 1937. Be that as it may, the Charleston is an integral and important part of the game that adds another layer of choices and decisions with which the player is confronted.

The function of the Charleston is to provide opportunities for the player to get rid of useless tiles and, hopefully, to receive useful ones. Most of the time, out of the twenty or so tiles you receive in the Charleston, at least one will turn out to be of value to your tentative choices. But the Charleston also provides opportunities to deny your opponents useful tiles and must also be viewed as a defensive strategy.

Let's explore this idea and discuss some definite "Dos and Don'ts."

First and foremost **never pass a Pair of any tile**. As you have probably learned by now, Pairs are the nemesis of many potential hands and you do not want to present your opponent with the gift of the Pair that may be needed in the Charleston. Additionally, the Pair could be helpful in completing a Pung or a Kong. If you have a Pair you can't use, break it up into separate passes. Don't help your opponents.

Next, don't pass Flowers. Unless you can't steal (blind pass) and have such good options for a hand you are desperate and have no other choice. The 2010 card had 27 hands that required Flowers—close to half. Again, don't help your opponents.

Pass disparate tiles, if it is possible. Passing a 3Bam and 5Bam might be helpful to an odd numbered or consecutive hand. But a 3Bam and a 7Dot, even though they are odd numbered tiles, usually are not. **And don't pass tiles all of the same Suit.**

Don't pass more than two different Wind tiles in one pass. Even though they are not a Pair, more than two Wind tiles can be the impetus for someone to start saving them for a hand, especially if you don't see them again in subsequent passes.

Often, the same tiles that have been passed come back around. You can be sure nobody needs them. Keep passing them and be assured you are not helping your opponents.

These tenets are basic to the Charleston.

WHAT TO KEEP?

Obviously, keep the tiles that strengthen or add to your hand. Or, as stated above, keep the tile that makes a Pair to start your hand.

Let's, theoretically say, you have tentatively focused in on several possible hands and are anxiously awaiting the start of the Charleston.

Let's look at an example of such a situation. Again, these examples reflect hands on the 2010 card.

2 66 8, 1 7 9, J, 3 5, N E, D

The Power is the Pair of **6Crak**, and a versatile Joker, useful in the even, 369, and Consecutive Run Sections.

Here are the hands on the card.

    222 4444, **666 8888** - even Section 7th hand
    FF 3333, **6666, 9999** -369 Section 3rd hand
    1111 **222** 3333 **DDD** - Consecutive Run Section 3rd hand
    FF 1111 **2222 3333** - Consecutive Run Section 5th hand

Here are my possible hands.

2 J(4), 66 8,	even - 5 tiles
3, **66,** 9J(9),	369 - 5 tiles
66, 7, 8, J(D)	consecutive - 5 tiles
5, **66,** 7J(7)	consecutive - 5 tiles

I have several good options so I will wait to see what the Charleston brings.
My first pass (first right) is the **1Dot**, **Green**, and **North**.
And I get a **4Dot**, a **7Bam**, and a **South**. I keep the **4Dot**.

Now the hands look like this:

2 4 J(4), 66 8 **+** 7Bam, S E
3, 66, 9J(9)
66, 7, 8, D(J)D
5, 66, 7(J)7

The second pass (opposite) is the **7Bam**, **East**, and the **South**.
I get an **8Bam**, **2Crak**, and a **1Dot**.
None of these tiles are useful.
Even though the 8Bam and the 2Crak are even numbered tiles, neither of these tiles is useful for the hands I have chosen. They are the wrong Suits. This demonstrates the important idea of only keeping the tiles that strengthen your Section and, in this case, the hand. These tiles are examples of "maybe" tiles. (See *What Not to Keep* below.)

I pass all of them, first left.
And I get another **4Dot**, an **8Crak** and a **1Bam**. Keep the **4Dot** and **8Crak**.

My hands now look like this.

2J(2) 44, 66 88 **+** 1Bam
3, 66, 9J(9)
66, 7, 8, D(J)
5, 66, 7(J)7

The even hand now has eight tiles toward a Mah Jongg as opposed to five tiles in the other Sections' hands, so this is my obvious choice of a hand to play. I now abandon the 369 and consecutive hands and use those tiles as part of the tiles I pass in the Charleston. Eight tiles toward Mah Jongg is a very good beginning hand.

Even Section 7th hand.

222 4444, 666 8888

My tiles.

2J(2) 44, 66 88 8 tiles

Here again, the Charleston has provided me with a definite hand to play.

And many times the Charleston provides you with two or more potential hands.

Here's an example.

F 1 5 7, J 7 99, 2 6 8 N D

Here are the Sections.

F 1 5 7, J 7 99,	8 odd
5 6 7, J 8, 99	7 consecutive run
F J 6, 99	6 369

The Power is the **Pair of 9Crak** and a useful **Joker**.

My first choice is the odd Section, the longest. My tiles are predominately "High" 5s, 7s, 9s, so the hand I consider is the 2nd "or" hand which uses the Power Pair but, unfortunately, does not require Flowers.

The Consecutive Run Section must be a second choice.

Here is the odd hand on the card.

    555 7777, 777 9999 2nd hand

Here are my tiles.

    5J(5)7, 7 99   5 tiles

Here are two Consecutive Run hands.

    111 2222 333 4444   2nd hand
    FF 1111 2222 3333   4th hand

Here are my tiles.

    6 7, J(8)99   5 tiles
    F 7J(7), 8,99   6 tiles

As the Charleston begins, I am looking for "high" odd numbers, 5 and 7Dots and 7 and 9Craks for the odd hand as well as 6Dots and 8Craks for the Consecutive hands.

The first right pass consists of the 1Dot, Soap, and the North.

I get an 8Crak, a Green, and a West.

Keep the 8Crak for the Consecutive Run hand.

6 7J(7), 8 99 + 2 D W
F 7J(7) 8,99

The second pass (opposite) reveals a 2Dot, 4Bam, and 3Crak. The 2Dot makes a Pair. The 2Dots are even and do not add to the odd numbered or consecutive hand. Pass one of them. You may be tempted to keep the 3Crak. The 3Crak is "low." You are looking for "high" numbers. Pass it.

The third pass (first left) gives me a 6Bam, a 5Crak, and a 2Bam.

Should you keep the 5Crak? Yes, it's a "high" number and closely related to the 7 and 9Crak and it might be useful later on for the 5th "or" odd numbered hand.

Here is the 5th "or" hand on the card.

FFFF 5555 77 9999

Here is my hand.

F J(5)5 7 99 + 2 6

The next three passes do not produce any other tiles for either hands.

The odd hands on the card.

555 777, 777 999   2nd "or" hand
FFFF 5555 77 9999   5th "or" hand

My tiles for the odd hands.

5J(5)7, 7 99   2nd "or" hand   6 tiles
F 5J(5) 7 99   5th "or" hand   6 tiles

Here are the Consecutive Run hands.

111 **2222 333 4444**   2nd hand
FF 1111 **2222 3333**   4th hand

Here are my tiles.

6 7J(7), 8 99   6 tiles
F 7J(7,) 8,99   6 tiles

All potential hands have six tiles toward Mah Jongg and one includes the Flower: two hands in the odd Section and two in the Consecutive Run Section.

And sometimes, the Charleston puts you on the horns of a dilemma.

Let's look at this example.

My tiles are

1 3, 1 3 7, 99, 2, 66, 8, D, W

The Power is **two Pairs: 6 and 9Bam**.

Let's find the Sections.

3, 3, 66 99	6	369 tiles
1 3, 1 3 7, 99	7	odd tiles
2 66 **8**	4	even tiles

In the odd Section, the predominance of numbers is "low" and these hands do not use both Power Pairs. The tiles fit better in the 369 Section because it uses both Power Pairs. The even Section is a non-starter. But let's see what the Charleston provides.

My first pass is the **2Dot**, **8Crak**, and **West**.

I get a **1Dot**, **2Bam**, and **Red**.

Keep the 1Dot. My hand looks like this:

1 3, 11 3 7, + 2, D D
3, 3, 66 99

As discussed above, on the 2010 card, there are no hands in the odd Section that use Dragons. But early in the Charleston, I am reluctant to break up either the 369 or the odd hand. Still, I have to pass three tiles. Since the 3s can be potentially useful for a 369 hand, I keep them and pass 1Crak, one of the Dragons (the Soap), and the 2Bam.

I get a **3Bam**, **5Dot**, and a **2Crak**. And yes, I keep the **3Bam** to use for a 369 hand and the **5Dot** for the odd hand.

My hand looks like this:

    3, 11 3 5, 7, + 2, D
    3 66 99,

On the 1st left pass, I pass the **7Dot**, **2Crak**, **Red** and I get another **5Dot**, **Green**, and **2Bam**

My hand now looks like this:

    11 3 55, 3 + 2
    3 66 99 D

Now I have two potential hands in two different Sections, the 369 and the odd.

Here is the 369 card's hand.

    3333 666 9999 DDD   1st hand

Here are my tiles.

3 66 99 D   6 tiles

Here is the hand in the odd Section: the 5th.

FFFF 1111 33 5555

Here are my tiles.

11 3 55   5 tiles

But I now have only two tiles to pass, the 3Crak and the 2Bam. I can't steal. What to do? Should I stop the Charleston? Which hand to pursue? Which hand to abandon?

The answer lies in the hands chosen from the card. Compare each hand on the card and determine which is the easier to complete.

What do I mean? The easiest hands are the ones that require no Pairs. The more difficult hands to make are the ones that require one or more Pairs. So determine which hand requires the fewer number of Pairs or the hand that requires no Pairs. Usually, choose the hand that requires no Pairs (or fewer Pairs) over the hand that requires one or more Pairs.

Besides the number of Pairs the hand requires, prefer the hand that has no "gaps," discussed above. Finally, Exposed hands are easier to make than Concealed hands.

So in the example above, choose the Exposed 369 hand, the longest, and which requires no Pairs over the odd hand which requires one Pair. Abandon the odd hand.

Note: In most instances, if you receive a tile that gives you the critical Pair your hand requires, choose that hand. If you already have the Pairs the hand requires, stay with that hand.

Let's look at another randomly chosen hand.

Here are my tiles.

F 1 2 6, 55, N EE W S, GG

The Winds-Dragons Section is clearly my choice. The Power is the Pair of **East**, the Pair of **Greens**, and the Pair of **5Craks** and the choice of hands is between the 3rd and the 5th.

Here are the hands on the card.

FFFF EEEE GG WWWW   3rd hand
NNN EW SSS 111 111   5th hand

Here are my tiles toward those hands.

F N EE W S 55 GG
F EE GG W   3rd hand 6 tiles
N EW S 55   5th hand 6 tiles

Even though both hands have the critical tiles, (the Pair of Green Dragons for the 3rd hand and the EW for the 5th) and they are equally strong, I choose the 3rd hand, because the 3rd hand has no gaps, (a Flower, two Easts, one West,) and, the final factor, is Exposed. The 5th hand is Concealed.

*A **cautionary note:** In the Charleston, keeping tiles to maintain options for other hands is reasonable and often players end up with two good potential hands. But as a novice, keeping too many options open is not a good idea and inevitably leads to confusion. When you have too many options available, making a decision about what tiles to keep and what tiles to pass finally becomes almost painful. More about this later.*

WHAT NOT TO KEEP

Obviously, tiles that do not advance or strengthen your hand.

The biggest mistake novice players make is to keep tiles received in the Charleston I call **"maybe" tiles**—tiles **unrelated** to your choice. "Maybe I can use this, if I change my hand." Or "Maybe I should keep this for later."

Once a hand is chosen, I caution novice players not to clutter their hands (or minds) with things that do not relate to it. "Maybe" tiles do nothing to strengthen the hand and keeping them leads to confusion, chaos, and indecision.

These are examples of "maybe" tiles.

❀   Your even numbered hand requires 2Bams and you get a 2Crak.

❀   Or you get a tile that matches a Suit, but not the numbers.

❀   Or you keep a Red Dragon when your hand requires Green Dragons.

❀   Or you get a tile that makes an extraneous Pair, a Pair that is not connected to or related to the Section or hand you have chosen. These Pairs are not "powerful." Again, a Pair is powerful only if it adds to your hand. Keeping a Pair that is foreign to your hand, just because it is a Pair, is usually not a good idea.

❀   As previously discussed, if you are looking for 5s, 7s, 9s, high numbers in the odd Section, don't be tempted to keep low numbers, 1s or 3s, even though they may be the correct Suits. The reverse is true. If you are looking for 1s, 3s, 5s, don't keep 7s or 9s.

Once you have six or seven or more tiles toward the hand you have chosen, stick to that hand. Until you gain a good deal of confidence and experience playing the game, stay with the original goals you have chosen. Even if you do not strengthen your choice of a hand in the Charleston, don't despair. The game is about to begin and opportunity to win abounds!

Let's summarize the ideas discussed.

SUMMARY

❀ Never pass a Pair of any tile. Break it up into two separate passes. Try not to pass two or more Winds together. Don't pass Flowers, unless you have no other choice. Don't pass tiles of the same Suit.

❀ Keep tiles that enhance your chosen hand.

❀ Keep tiles that are closely related to your choice for an "option."

❀ Don't keep "maybe" tiles that do not strengthen or are not related to your choice.

❀ An extraneous Pair that has no connection to your hand(s) is not useful, nor "Powerful."

❀ When deciding between two hands, choose the easier hand. Abandon the tiles for the more difficult hand.
   Easier hands are
   a) Exposed vs. Concealed
   b) Require no Pairs vs. one or more Pairs or the hand that requires the fewer number of Pairs. If you already have the Pairs required, stay with that hand.
   c) Count the number of tiles toward Mah Jongg in each hand.
      Choose the longer, stronger hand.
   d) Choose the hand that has no "gaps."

You can see that some of the criteria useful in selecting your hand are the same that are useful in the Charleston. And now we're going to see that, again, some of them are useful for the next chapter, *Let the Game Begin!* But before going on to the next Chapter, use all the ideas we discussed and do the Practice exercise on the next page.

PRACTICE

Since finding your hand and the Charleston are "companion" procedures, after you've done the Practice exercise recommended in the previous Chapter, do the Charleston. Take three tiles from your hand and replace them with three random tiles from the table, six times and then do a Courtesy. If you pick a Joker, (that's a no no) put it back and select another tile. I suggest you do the same if you pick a Flower, since you probably won't get a Flower (or a Pair) passed to you in the Charleston.

Let the Game Begin!

Your goal in Mah Jongg is, of course, to win. But don't forget you have another goal as well—to keep your opponents from winning. And for you to reach either or both goals, you need a firm grasp of the hands and good decisions based on the knowledge derived from the evidence presented to you by the discards, the Exposures, and the proximity to the end of the game.

We will see the strategies you employ as the game begins are not the same as the ones you employ as the game progresses and will change, as circumstances change, and change again as the game is coming to an end.

For example, in the beginning of the game, discarding usually does not present a problem. Mostly, no one calls for discards early, probably because the hand is not yet definitely decided, the combinations are incomplete, or early Exposures are not a good idea, as we will soon discuss. But as the game progresses and as players begin to expose, discarding becomes more important and now playing defensively becomes the critical component of your game to keep your opponents from winning. So we'll first discuss some discarding procedures, then cover topics that deal with Exposures and their significance to your strategy, and finally, when to change the hand and to which hand to change—all closely affecting your defensive play.

Before we begin the discussion of specific strategies, one issue, seemingly trivial, is one that is not actually trivial at all. Many novice players find it easier to "see" the hand by leaving spaces between each combination required separately on the rack. This is a sign of an inexperienced player. Savvy players can tell how close you are to Mah Jongg when you have your discards separate from the rest of your tiles at the end of your rack. Or if you keep one tile separated from the rest of your tiles, it's not hard to figure out you are waiting to complete a Pair and so on.

Don't separate your tiles into Pairs, Pungs, Kongs, and discards by leaving spaces in between them on your rack. Don't give your hand away.

The first defensive strategy is the simplest and easiest that many players are not aware of or choose to ignore. Look at the back of your card. It's #5.

What is "Racking"? It's immediately placing the tile you have just picked from the Wall onto your rack, next to the other tiles.

Why is it important? Because once you have "racked," you have removed the opportunity for an opponent to call for the discarded tile he or she may need, for anything. It may be an Exposure tile or a Mah Jongg tile, and the longer you hold on to the just picked tile before you rack it, the more time another player has to call for the previously discarded tile.

Once you pick a tile, don't turn it right-side up so you can see it. Don't hold it in your hand while you decide whether to keep it or discard it. Just put it on your rack. Once the tile is racked, then there is time for you to decide. Picking a tile and immediately racking it is good defensive play.

Note: Tapping the tile on top of the rack is not racking.

There is a controversy about racking. Experienced players tend to rack quickly and to play quickly. They have a thorough knowledge of the hands and what hands they have options for and are quick to make decisions. Novice players often complain that if the tile is racked quickly, it doesn't allow them enough time to decide to call for the just discarded tile. Perhaps, as a novice player, you find yourself in this situation. Regrettably, there is no magic solution. It will help if you stop the game quickly and then you can consider whether to call or not. (Saying "Uh" doesn't always do it.) Say "Wait!" "Hold!" "Stop!" or anything else to stop the game before the next player picks and racks a tile. It may take several games for you to speed up "racking" and quicken decision making.

And then there are those who claim that racking slows down the game. I do not agree. I have yet to see that racking slows the game.

Racking is a legitimate defensive move and does what it is designed to do—keep opponents from calling a tile they need. If you choose to ignore it, you are not availing yourself of a powerful defensive strategy.

DISCARDS

Keep track of the discards, not only of the tiles you need, but of the tiles others are discarding. As the game progresses and Exposures are made, it is one of the important factors in helping to determine what is a "safe" tile, a "hot" tile, (see below), the hands your opponents may be playing and when you find you need to change your hand, remembering what tiles for the new hand have already been discarded. It can be critical in your decision.

A Caveat: Many novice players give up on the hand just because one or two needed tiles are discarded, especially in the early stages of the game. Rememb , there are four of each tile, eight Flowers, and eight Jokers. The chances of picking needed tiles from the Wall are good. Don't despair. Your hand is not Dead yet! But once the tiles you need for a Pair are discarded, you will have to make adjustments. More about this later.

"SAFE" TILES

What is a safe tile? A tile the opponents do not or cannot call. Keeping track of the discards helps assure that your discards are safe. If a tile is discarded and no one calls it, discard the same tile again as soon as possible. It is probably safe. Besides being safe, when a player needs that tile for a combination but cannot (or does not) call it, you have reduced the possibility of that player being able to win by repeatedly discarding the needed tile.

A Note: What was once a safe tile does not always remain a safe tile. A player may have waited for a second or third discard to call for that tile. Or did not have enough tiles to complete the combination, but now has.

Discard Flowers early in the game, once you're sure you don't need them. The 2010 card had over 10 hands that require a Kong of Flowers. It's usually reasonable to expect players don't have enough Flowers early in the game to complete a Kong. (Some older cards required a couple of hands that required a Sextet of Flowers). And calling a discarded Flower for a Pair (and Mahj) early in the game is unlikely.

"HOT" TILES

A hot tile is a tile that has not been discarded during the game or a tile you have determined a player needs for an Exposure or for Mah Jongg. It is a potentially dangerous discard. That's why it's hot.

In the beginning of the game, your discard, most likely, is not hot. But as the game progresses, making that determination becomes more critical. For example, if you can count two 6Dots already discarded, a third discard is probably safe. But if you can see none or just one 6Dot, your discard is probably less safe. That's why you need to keep track of the discards.

Don't discard Flowers late in the game. At the end of the game they are "hot," even if you can account for six or seven of them. On the 2010 card, 11 hands required a Kong of Flowers, for which Jokers can be used. And there were 11 hands that required a Pair of Flowers, and that doesn't include the Singles and Pairs Section. At the end of the game, waiting for a Flower to complete a Pair for Mahj is not unusual. That's why discarding them early is a good idea, but not at the end of the game.

As a matter of fact, once there are only two or three picks left in the Wall, almost any tile, hot or not, is a potential Mahj tile for an opponent. Since you can't see others' hands you don't always know what someone else's Mahj tile may be. You don't know how many Jokers an opponent may have to complete some needed combination and what was once a "safe" tile now has the potential to be a "hot" tile. Protect yourself and keep your opponents from Victory. Play defensively: if you must, break up your hand, and discard the safest tiles of all, Jokers.

I can empathize with players' reluctance to discard their powerful Jokers at the end of the game. But you are discarding them because they are no longer useful to your hand. When you are two or more tiles away from winning and there are just two or three picks left, Jokers will not magically get you any closer to Mahj. Regrettably, your chances of winning are essentially zero.

Now you should think of them as "Guardians" to protect you from the angst and penalty of providing Mahj to someone else. Be resolved—when Jokers are no longer useful to your hand, you need to use them to protect you. You must break up your hand and discard Jokers.

Or do you? The game is coming to an end and there are two or three picks left in the Wall and you are one tile away and "waiting" to declare Mah Jongg yourself. The question now becomes, should you hope to Mahj or should you break up your hand and play defensively?

Will someone discard your Mah Jongg tile? Probably not. Your opponents will not (or should not) discard hot tiles or any tiles at the end of the game. From the Exposures and discards, the other players have probably determined your hand and will not discard your Mah Jongg tile. Even if there are no Exposures, they will be playing defensively and discarding Jokers.

What is the possibility of picking the Mah Jongg tile? Does hope spring eternal? In American Mah Jongg,

I don't think so. The chances of picking your Mah Jongg tile are again almost zero. Rarely does the Mahj tile turn up at the end of the game. In over 15 years of playing Mah Jongg, I have experienced once that I have picked the last Wall tile for Mah Jongg. And I have seen two other times that another player picked the Mah Jongg tile at the end of the game. Again, a critical choice is necessary. Do you hope to win or do you keep others from winning? My answer is "Play defensively." Keep others from winning. Break up your hand. Discard Jokers.

DISCARDS AND EXPOSURES

Once the Exposures of an opponent disclose the hand requires a Pair of something, discard that tile as soon as you can and hope it is not called for Mahj. If it isn't, an immediate second discard is almost surely safe. Discarding tiles for a Pair an opponent needs as early in the game as possible is a sure way to keep that player from winning. More about this later.

As the game progresses, from the Exposures you have determined what hand is being played by an opponent and you are fairly sure you have the Mahj tile. Don't keep it "for later." Eventually you will have to discard it, if you want to win. Discard it earlier in the game and hope your opponent is not ready to Mahj. The later in the game you discard it, the chances are greater that your opponent will call it for Mahj.

WHAT IF A PLAYER DISCARDS A JOKER?

Obviously, it's an unneeded tile. It's a clue that he or she is close to Mah Jongg, waiting for a tile to complete a Pair, playing a Singles and Pairs hand or is trying for a Jokerless hand. Check the Exposures, the tiles already discarded, and be very judicious about your discards. And be even more observant of what tiles the player has or is discarding.

Discard tip: When you have a Pair of something you cannot use, discard one and hope someone calls it and exposes, using a Joker. When it's your turn, you can now exchange the second tile for the Joker. Sometimes this works but sometimes the player waits for the second discard and then calls.

A caveat about exchanging a Joker with a missing tile in an Exposure: It's usually to your advantage to exchange an exposed Joker for the missing tile. But not always. Since you can't see the hand an opponent is playing, you may be helping the opponent toward a Jokerless hand when you make the exchange. Or you find you can't use the exchanged Joker, because all you need to complete your hand is a tile for a Pair. The Joker is of no use to your hand but the exchange can potentially help your opponent.

EXPOSURES

When to expose, when not to expose—a big question whose decision often determines the outcome of a game.

Exposing is fun, but like lots of fun things, it comes at a price. And the price you pay is that you are freely giving away important information to your opponents about your hand. One Exposure probably will not give your hand away, but it can eliminate a huge part of the card. There are only a limited number of hands that could fit your Exposure. Savvy players will be sure to make initial deductions from it. The more Exposures you make, the easier it will be to determine the hand you are playing. Once you have given away this critical information, your opponents will thank you for your generosity by making sure they do not discard other tiles you need or discard other needed tiles before you can call.

So, expose only when you must!

That means call to expose only when there is no other option left, especially early in the game. Early detection is a plus for some things, like a terrorist plot, but not for Mah Jongg. Early detection can prove to be fatal!

48

Let's discuss some typical situations.

The game has started and you are looking for a tile to complete a Pung. The needed tile is discarded. Your instinct is to call it. My advice is to wait. Instant gratification can be satisfying, but in Mah Jongg, not good strategy. "But what if I never see the tile again?" You'd be surprised how many times you "see the tile again" or pick the tile yourself that keeps you from having to expose. And, remember, there are eight Jokers. And if your Pung contains a Joker and one or two of your tiles go out, there is still one more left. Since it wasn't called the first two times, the probability of someone discarding it again is great. Then call. And your Joker will not be vulnerable to be exchanged by another player.

In this scenario, you are waiting to complete a Kong. If you already have the three natural tiles you need, of course, call for the fourth. In this case you must call to expose. But if your potential Kong contains a Joker, wait for the fourth tile to be discarded. Again, you could pick the tile or another Joker yourself or exchange a tile for an exposed Joker. Further, once the tiles that could be exchanged for your Joker are discarded, it is safe from being a potential plus for someone else.

But be aware, this can be a double-edged sword! When your Exposure does contain a Joker, it is vulnerable to be exchanged for the missing tile by another player. On the other hand, it's not unusual to pick the missing tile yourself, allowing for the opportunity to exchange the tile for your own Joker, strengthening your own hand.

Let's talk about exposing Flowers. Novice players are anxious to call them, for example, particularly for hands on the 2010 card because all the Exposures had to be Kongs. Remember there are eight Flowers and eight Jokers—16 possible chances to complete the Flower combination needed for your hand. When they are being freely discarded, players will assume they are a safe discard. Don't be tempted to call the first or the second discarded Flower. Keep count of how many Flowers are out and how many are left. Wait until you must call. And chances of picking the needed Flowers yourself are great.

Early in the game, especially if your chosen hand has Jokers but is fairly weak, (has gaps, is missing needed Pairs, has only five or six tiles) it is not a good idea to expose them all in one combination. It can strip your hand of the strength they have added to it, leaving you unable to make other Exposures or complete other combinations. Again, wait to expose until your hand is stronger, or you have enough tiles to keep your hand viable. Remember you should have at least seven or eight tiles toward Mah Jongg before you call and expose. Additionally, an early Exposure may reveal your hand or tiles an opponent needs for a Pair. He or she now has a good opportunity to change the hand and perhaps to declare Mah Jongg.

So, distribute your Joker strength.

What do I mean?

Let's say you have two Jokers, one tile toward a Pung and two tiles toward a Kong. If you use one Joker with the Kong and one with the Pung, both combinations are then waiting to be completed or exposed. Using both Jokers with either the Pung or Kong, weakens the other. Distributing Joker power adds strength to your hand.

Weak or not, don't expose until you are fairly certain of the choice of the hand you are playing, because once you expose, you have made a strong commitment to that particular hand. So unless you are sure of your choice, **wait** until you are, even if tiles you could use are discarded. Too often I've seen the player who exposes before the hand is solidly decided lose. Avoid lamenting, "I should have waited."

As the game progresses, the urgency to call for Exposures increases. Be sure you keep count of the tiles you need that have been discarded so you know when you have to call to complete your combinations. But now, the closer to the end of the game, the more reasonable it becomes to expose more than one Joker in a combination, or make a second or even a third Exposure. With two Exposures, you have revealed the one or two possible hands you are playing. Three Exposures leave no doubt. (See *Reading Exposures*, below.) Just be prepared for the others to make it very difficult for you to win.

READING EXPOSURES

In the first Chapter, I suggested studying your card to determine what its particular characteristics were to help you find a hand. Now the study has another benefit—a larger one. In order to defend skillfully and successfully, it is critical to know what hands your opponents are pursuing, and the knowledge gained from your study is an invaluable and essential tool in determining what information the Exposures have revealed.

In your study, look, for example, for which and how many hands require Pungs or Kongs of Flowers, which and how many hands require Dragon combinations, Pungs vs. Kongs of specific numbers and Winds, combinations required in Concealed hands, etc. Match your knowledge of the hands to the Exposures and you have a big heads-up in determining the opponent's hand.

Exposures are "tell-alls" and expose the hand. Maybe that's another reason they are called "Exposures." Although one Exposure may not lead to the specific hand a player may be pursuing, because many hands require the same tiles, it can narrow the search down considerably.

Each Exposure offers specific "clues," available for all to see. The number one tool to uncover these clues is how thoroughly you have studied the card. Your ability to spot the specific information the Exposure has given is the key to how you decide to play offensively and defensively.

What are these clues?

The first clue is **What is the Exposure: a Pung, Kong, Quint?**

 Let's take an example of an Exposure of a Pung of 2s.

The hands will again reference the 2010 card, but you can use these examples as you study your current card.

I started by looking for how many hands on the card required a Pung of 2s. The count immediately began in the 2468 Section, but my close examination revealed there is only one even hand, the 7th, that requires a Pung of 2s. All the others hands require either a Pair or a Kong. Next, in the Consecutive Run Section, there were possibly two hands that required a Pung of 2s, the 2nd and 3rd. The other Sections in which a Pung of 2s could be used were the Like Numbers Sections, the 2nd hand, and the 3rd hand in the 2010 Section. So out of the more than 50 hands on the card there were only six that could use a Pung of 2s.

But the situation changed considerably if the Exposure was a Kong of 2s, because close examination revealed there were 12 hands that either required a Kong of 2s or could use a Kong of 2s.

The second clue is **What kind of number is the Exposure—odd or even?**

Generally, the Sections that can use an odd number are 13579, Consecutive Run, and, on some cards, Like Numbers: for even numbers it's the 2468, Consecutive Run, and Like Numbers Sections.

But sometimes the specific number can be of value to find the hand. For example, on the 2010 card: a Pung of 9s was found in only two hands: the 2nd Like Numbers hand or as an "option" for the 5th 13579 hand. A Pung of 8s was found in four hands: the 2nd Like Numbers hand and the 1st, 2nd, and 3rd Consecutive Run hand. Surprise! None in the 2468 Section. The last hand, the 8th, was Concealed.

The third clue is **Is the Exposure a Flower, Dragon, or Wind?**

Winds are easy: Winds, Dragons, and the Quint Sections were the only hands that required Wind Exposures on the 2010 card. The last "Year" hand was Concealed.

On the 2010 card, an Exposure of Dragons was not from the odd Section. And there were only four Exposed hands that required a Pung of Dragons, the 2nd Like Numbers hand, the 3rd Consecutive Run hand, and the 1st and 5th 369 hands. Kongs of Dragons were required in five hands. Flowers were found all over the card in every Section. They were all Kongs.

But in many cases, a player makes a second Exposure and this time the hand is almost surely identifiable or is one of two possible hands.

More critical clues are available.

The number of Suits—one or two, and the kinds of numbers on the tiles: even, odd, consecutive, 369, etc. make it easier to determine the hands.

Let's look at examples of two one-Suited Exposures.

555 7777— a Pung of 5 and a Kong of 7 odd numbers.

The hands with two one-Suited Exposures are easier to determine because generally, there are only two or three hands in the four most often encountered Sections that require two one-Suited Exposures. In our example, the numbers are a Pung and a Kong of odd numbers and the hand was found in the odd Section: the 2nd "or" hand.

555 7777 777 9999

Example:

4444 5555 – 2 Kongs of consecutive numbers.

The Consecutive Section is obviously where to look. There are a limited number of hands in that Section that require two Exposures in one Suit and whether the Exposures are Pungs or Kongs will reveal the hand. This one happens to be the 4th hand.

FFFF 1111 2222 DD

Here's another.

666 8888 – a Pung and a Kong of even numbers.

The 2010 card's even and Consecutive Run Sections had several hands with two one-Suit Exposures, and once again, the combinations of the Exposures, Pungs, or Kongs reveal which hand it is. This Exposure is from the even Section: #7.

222 4444 666 8888

Let's look at two Exposures in two different Suits. Again the hands reference the 2010 card as examples.

333, 666 - a Pung of 3s and a Pung of 6s.

The two Sections that can use 3s and 6s together are the 369 and the Consecutive Run.
 The 369 Section had the only hand that uses a Pung of 3s and a Pung of 6s in two Suits: the 2nd hand.

333 6666 666 9999

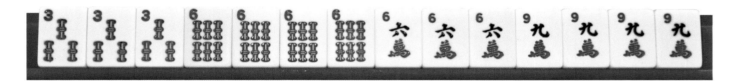

It can't be in the Consecutive Run Section, because the only hand it could be was the 2nd and the 6s had to be a Kong.

111 2222 333 4444

Let's study another typical Exposure.

5555 DDD—a Kong of 5Dots and a Pung of Red.

You might think of the odd Section, but as pointed out before, the 2010 card has no hands in that Section that require Dragons. The Consecutive Section or Like Numbers are the only other choices. It could be either the 3rd. Consecutive Run or the 2nd Like Numbers hand.

1111 222 3333 DDD

11 DD 111 DDD 1111

How can you tell which one it is? You can't for sure. But you have some clues to the hand in front of you. Check the discards and observe what the player is discarding. If 4Craks or 3Dots are out, assume the Like Numbers hand. If other 5s are discarded, (for the Like Numbers hand) assume the Consecutive Run hand.

Let's do one more.

444, 666—a Pung of 4s and 6s.

The 2468 and Consecutive Run are the two Sections to consider. In this case, there were two hands that use this combination of Exposures, the 2nd hand in the even Section or the 2nd Consecutive Run hand.

111 2222 333 4444

22 444 44 666 8888

In the Exposures above, if 5Dots or 7Craks are out it's probably the even hand. If three 2Dots are out, the opponent either has to change the hand or lose. (The hand requires a Pair of 2Dots.)

Here is a situation that you will no doubt encounter at some time that involves everything discussed so far.

The Scenario: Player A has revealed the hand through the Exposures and you have determined the hand requires a Pair. Two of the tiles for the Pair are already discarded. You have picked the third tile. And you know the player can't win without that tile. Should you discard it?

No, if the game is close to the end. Your opponent cannot win but neither can you.

And yes, if the game is in the early-to-middling stages. But how early? It's reasonable to expect the player isn't ready to Mahj if the game is just about half over (discussed below in *Changing Your Hand*). But the longer you keep it, the greater the chance of the hand being set to Mahj.

But since you are close to Mahj yourself, you take a chance and discard it. To your relief, the player doesn't call it. You may now challenge the player and declare the hand "Dead" because the rule is if three tiles for a required Pair are discarded, the hand cannot be made. Therefore the player is disqualified from the game and the hand declared "Dead."

It's to your advantage to declare your opponent's hand Dead because playing with three players as opposed to four increases your chances of picking tiles you need by twenty-five percent.

We've all heard the expression "The best offence is a good defense." Nothing is truer than that advice in Mah Jongg. Playing defensively is just as important, and many times more important, as playing to win. And keep in mind, the closer to the end of the game, the more defensively you must play. In the beginning of this book, I said experienced players were often regarded as "great." They are "great" because they are strong defensive players. Their "secrets of success" are they know the hands, they quickly determine others' hands, and once that determination is made, they use every defensive strategy available to keep their opponents from winning. One of their "secrets" is defensive playing.

So study your card! Use the clues discussed, because determining the hands others are playing influences not only decisions about your own hand, but once you discover the hand opponents are playing, the specific defensive decisions you choose become the key to winning or losing and to "greatness."

CHANGING YOUR HAND

In many games, the need or desire to change a hand occurs. As circumstances change, so might your hand. It's a frequently occurring phenomenon. So "I might play this hand if this tile comes in or play this hand if that tile comes in" is quite sensible, especially when you have good options from which to choose.

But, as I tell my students, "You can't keep everything." Ultimately, a decision has to be made and one hand must be chosen and the other abandoned—if you want to win. Again, this is a critical decision.

When to change the hand and to which hand to change become the questions the player frequently confronts. It's not always a simple or easy decision. Weighing the pros and cons of each option can end up with seemingly distressing choices and sometimes you find yourself on the horns of a dilemma.

And unfortunately, there is usually not a lot of time to make the decision. Mah Jongg is the most fun when the game moves at a fairly crisp pace. Saying "Wait a minute" while you ponder whether you should call a tile for one hand vs. another is usually not much fun for you or your opponents and halts the smooth flow of the game. It also reveals information about a hand you might be considering, again giving away valuable information to your opponents for free. And finally, it reveals a fundamental weakness in your game: that your knowledge of the hands is fragile.

Fortunately, there are guidelines you can use to help determine when to change your hand and to which potential hand to change. These guidelines will be the focus of the next sections.

WHEN TO CHANGE YOUR HAND

"Timing is everything." We all have heard that familiar cliché. But it's true, especially in Mah Jongg. Changing your hand too early in the game or too late in the game can lead to a loss.

What is too early? The game has begun and is in the early stages or not yet half over (see below) and, regrettably, a couple of your needed tiles have already been discarded. Just because one or two of your needed tiles are discarded early, don't abandon your hand too soon! Remember there are four of each tile and eight Jokers in the game so the chances of picking your needed tiles are not over.

What is too late? The deciding factor is whether there are enough tiles left in the Wall for you to have a reasonable chance to create a winning hand. What is reasonable? If the game is about half over, you probably still have enough picks from the Wall. But if two Walls are gone and well into the third, it's probably too late to change your hand and hope to win.

Let's get a little technical here to determine what is "half-over." There are 152 tiles in a Mah Jongg set—52 tiles make up the 4 hands of the players (13x4). That leaves 100 tiles left for picking. Each player gets $^1/_4$ of those picks or 25 new tiles, give or take two or three. When the game is about half over, 50 or so tiles have been picked and discarded, leaving about 50 more. On average, that equates to around one full Wall (38 tiles) plus the tiles in East's Wall (average of about 10-12 tiles). Out of the 50 or so new tiles, you have about 10-12 chances to pick and/or call what are the needed tiles for a new hand. Allowing that none of your needed tiles are not already discarded, the chances of creating a new hand are about fifty-fifty. But after that, the opportunities rapidly decline.

Keeping in mind the discussion above, here are some common circumstances that signal a need to change your hand.

You need to change your hand when

❀ **The game is about half over and your hand is not improving.**
As the game progresses, if one or two of your needed tiles are not already discarded, entertain the possibility that some other player may also be saving the same tiles.

❀ **Your needed tiles are discarded before you can call because your combinations are incomplete, your hand is not strong enough to call, or your hand is Concealed.**

❀ **An opponent's Exposure reveals tiles you need, especially for a Pair.**

❀ **Three tiles you need for a Pair are discarded before you are ready to declare Mah Jongg.**
There's not much you can do in this instance. But sometimes, you can change your hand to one that doesn't require the Pair or, if the hand requires a Pair and a Pung, you can switch the Pair to a Pung or the Pung to a Pair.

❀ **You have made an erroneous Exposure.**
You have made an Exposure for a Concealed hand. Other errors might be that you have exposed a Pung instead of a Kong or vise versa or exposed the wrong number or Suit.

If and when you realize your mistake, look for another hand, **quietly**, that uses your Exposure, most likely in the Section your Exposure is in or in one that fits the tiles you have exposed. Look for alternate hands before it is your turn to pick from the Wall because when you say "Wait a minute," and scramble around looking for a hand, you are holding up the game and the other players will quickly become aware of your dilemma. If there isn't an alternative hand or you can't find one, keep playing anyway. Do not announce your mistake to the others, because it gives the advantage to your opponents of more picks from the Wall and greater chances of winning. If you are challenged by a sharp opponent, you may suffer the consequence of your hand being declared "Dead" and paying the challenger a monetary penalty.

WHICH HAND TO CHOOSE

There are many times a player has two good potential hands and as the game progresses, must decide between them.

Here again are some of the same criteria used when you first selected your hand and then again, decided what tiles to keep or pass in the Charleston.

❀ **Count the number of tiles toward Mah Jongg. Choose the hand that has the greater number.**

Abandon one hand when

❀ **You pick a tile that determines which of two hands to play, particularly if you pick the tile for a crucial Pair.**

❀ **Choose an Exposed hand over a Concealed hand.**

❀ **Check the Exposures and discards.**
If the tiles you need are exposed in another player's hand, especially for a Pair, choose the alternative.

And here is the most important and critical and number one factor of all:

❀ **Choose the hand that requires no Pairs over the hand that requires one or more Pairs.**

✿ **Or choose the hand that requires the fewest number of Pairs.**

Pairs are the number one "make or break" factor of many hands. So I repeat, as the game progresses if the hand requires a Pair that you don't already have and you do not pick the tile or once you see the tiles go out, you obviously need to change your hand.

But, in general, do not change your hand once you have the tiles for the Pairs you need. Stay with that hand.

There are some factors we discussed that need a little further discussion which are directly related to these two frequently occurring decisions of when and to which hands to change.

We discussed keeping your options open and it is reasonable and a productive idea to have Plan "B" ready if Plan "A" fails. In Mah Jongg, thinking ahead is an important and vital skill. But having plan "C," "D," and "E" as options is not reasonable, nor productive. Having too many options available creates havoc and it is a recipe for loss. Making a final decision about which option is best becomes almost impossible and usually by the time a final decision is made, the needed tiles are out and it's too late in the game to win.

Another caveat about changing the hand: avoid excessive hand-changing. Picking a tile for this hand, changing the hand, picking a tile for that hand, changing your hand again, over and over is a common error that many unseasoned players make. I'm not suggesting it's not reasonable to change your hand when you pick new tiles that offer a new, stronger alternate hand. But don't keep tiles for every alternative possible. It will lead to confusion and chaos.

But there are times that frequently changing your hand does lead to a win. These instances are rare and you need a lot of experience to bring one of these hands to fruition. As you gain experience, you will begin to better assess these situations and be more confident about deciding which hand shows the greatest promise.

In all of the situations we have discussed above, keep one more thing in mind. As you play, as long as you have tiles to discard, you can keep your options open. It's only when "decision" time is at hand that you must make the final choice of which hand to keep and which hand to abandon.

And finally, in any situation, when you find you can't win, you must **play defensively**. Hopefully, the value of keeping track of the discards to help you discern which tiles are safe and which are hot has become evident. Breaking up your hand and discarding Jokers, discussed above, can be a sorrowful situation but a necessary one.

In my strategy classes, players often voiced concern that they were "stuck"—they felt constrained to playing the few hands they were "comfortable" with. Playing hands out of their comfort zone made them apprehensive. And the question to me was "What can I do?"

I assured them that playing an unfamiliar hand, like trying anything unfamiliar, can produce discomfort. It's only natural. Staying with the few "old reliables" only reinforced their anxiety to try new ones. We all know the more familiar you become with something new, the less anxious you are with it—just like playing an unfamiliar hand. So my suggestion was, don't avoid unfamiliar hands. Play them, even though it creates discomfort, no matter if you win or lose. It gets easier.

If your goal is to be a proficient Mah Jongg player, study the card and its anomalies and if necessary, memorize it. Yes, it can be tedious and time-consuming. But, the rewards justify the effort because all the challenges of the game, from the first peek at the tiles to the declaration of "Mah Jongg!" depend on how well you know the hands on the card. There is no substitute for this Number One vital skill—whether you are playing to win or playing defensively!

By now, you can see that everything you do hinges on the information acquired and the consequential decisions and strategies we have discussed. And yet, no matter how skillful a player you are, it seems there are days, weeks, and sometimes months at a time you cannot lose. The Mah Jongg Fairies are smiling. And there are days, weeks, and months you cannot win. It feels like the Mah Jongg Forces are against you. Don't despair. I guarantee "This, too, shall pass." Until then, have fun and take heart. My parting words are

MAY THE TILES BE WITH YOU!

P.S. After you have finished the Quiz, you might want to read the articles about some little known aspects of Mah Jongg that may add another dimension to and a deeper appreciation of the game.

Tape this edge
to the other
red-starred
edge.

OFFICIAL STANDARD HANDS AND RULES

$7.00

2009
麻雀

NATIONAL
MAH JONGG
LEAGUE, INC.

72nd Year

Copyright © National Mah Jongg League, Inc. 2009 US and Canada.
All Rights Reserved. The right to reproduce any part of this document is unlawful.

This copy of the National Mah Jongg League's copyrighted
Card of Hands for 2009 is used here, with generous permission,
for learning purposes only. You may not duplicate it.

*Cut out the two pieces of the card (found here and on the next page)
and tape them together.*

NOTE: WHITE DRAGON IS USED AS ZERO "0". IT MAY BE USED WITH ANY SUIT.
(CRAKS, BAMS OR DOTS)

2009   VALUES

NNNN EW SSSS 2009 (Any 2 and 9 Same Suit) . . . . **X 25**
FF 2009 9999 9999 (Any 3 Suits, Kong 9s Only) . . . . **X 30**
FF GGGG 2009 RRRR (Kong Green & Red Dr. Only. Any 2 & 9 Same Suit) . . **X 35**
FFFF 22 000 000 99 (Any 2 and 9 Same Suit) . . . . **X 40**

2468

FF 2222 44 66 8888 (Any 2 Suits) . . . . **X 25**   ★
2222 4444 6666 88 . . . . **X 25**   ★
22 44 444 666 8888 (Any 3 Suits) . . . . **X 25**   ★
FFFF 222 888 DDDD . . . . **X 25**
222 444 6666 8888 (Any 2 Suits) . . . . **X 25**
FFFF 4444 X 6666 = 24 or **FFFF 6666 X 8888 = 48** . . . . . **X 30**
222 44 666 888 888 (Any 3 Suits, Pung 8s only) . . . . **C 35**

SEVEN HANDS

FFFF 3333 + 8888 =11 or **FFFF 3333 + 8888 =11** (Any 3 Suits) . . . **X 25**
FFFF 4444 + 7777 =11 or **FFFF 4444 + 7777 =11** (Any 3 Suits) . . . **X 25**
FFFF 5555 + 6666 =11 or **FFFF 5555 + 6666=11** (Any 3 Suits) . . . **X 25**

Tape this edge
to the other
blue-starred
edge.

WINDS - DRAGONS

	VALUES
NN EEE FFFF WWW SS	X 25
NNNN EEEE WWWW SS	X 25
NNNN 111 111 SSSS (Pung Any Like Odd No. in One Suit Only)	X 30
EEEE 222 222 WWWW (Pung Any Like Even No. in One Suit Only)	X 30
FF DDDD NEWS DDDD (Kong Any 2 Dragons)	X 25
FFFF DDD DDDD DDD (Any 3 Suits)	X 30

369

	VALUES
FFFF 3333 66 9999	X 25
333 666 6666 9999 (Any 2 Suits)	X 25
33 66 99 3333 3333 (Any 3 Suits; Like Kongs 3, 6 or 9)	X 25
33 666 DDDD 666 99 (Any 3 Suits)	X 25
FF 3333 6666 9999 (Any 3 Suits)	X 25
FF 33 66 99 DDD DDD (Any 3 Suits)	X 35
FF 333 666 999 999 (Any 3 Suits)	C 35

SINGLES AND PAIRS

	VALUES
FF NN EW SS 11 11 11 (Any Like No.)	C 50
FF 11 22 33 44 55 DD (Any 5 Consec. Nos. Pr. Like Dr.)	C 50
FF 22 44 66 88 22 22 (Any Like Even Pr. in Other 2 Suits)	C 50
11 33 55 77 99 11 11 (Any Like Odd Pr. in Other 2 Suits)	C 50
223 22334 223344 (Start same No. Any 3 Consec. Nos: Any 3 Suits)	C 50
FF 2009 NEWS 2009 (1 or 2 Suits, 2 and 9 Same Suit)	C 75

QUINTS

	VALUES
1123 11111 11111 (Any 3 Consec. Nos; Pr. Any No. in Run; Pr. & Quints Match)	X 40
11111 2222 33333 (Any 3 Consecutive Nos.)	X 40
FFFF NNNNN 11111 (Quint Any Wind & Any No. in Any Suit)	X 40
111 3333 55555 DD or 555 7777 99999 DD	X 45

CONSECUTIVE RUN

	VALUES
11 222 3333 444 55 or 55 666 7777 888 99	X 25
111 222 3333 4444 (Any 2 Suits, Any 4 Consecutive Nos.)	X 25
1111 22 22 22 3333 (Any 3 Consec. Nos. Like Prs. Middle No. Only)	X 30
11 22 111 222 DDDD (Any 3 Suits; Any 2 Consec. Nos. Kong Dr. 3rd Suit)	X 25
FF 1111 2222 3333 (Any 3 Suits; Any 3 Consec. Nos.)	X 25
11 22 333 DDD DDD DDD (Any 3 Suits; Any 3 Consec. Nos. Pung Opp. Dragons)	C 35

13579

	VALUES
11 333 5555 777 99	X 25
FFFF 1111 9999 DD	X 25
11 33 111 333 5555 or 55 77 555 777 9999 (Any 3 Suits)	X 25
FFFF 1111 33 5555 or FFFF 5555 77 9999	X 25
11 333 DDDD 333 55 (Any 3 Suits)	X 25
55 777 DDDD 777 99 (Any 3 Suits)	X 25
1111 33 55 77 9999 (Any 3 Suits)	X 30
111 3 555 555 7 999 (Any 2 Suits)	C 35

★ ★ ★

Tape this edge to the other blue-starred edge.

When a player Mah Jongs on a discarded tile, **DISCARDER** pays the winner double value. All other players pay single value. When a player picks OWN Mah Jongg tile, all players pay double value.

BONUS: WHEN A PLAYER DECLARES MAH JONGG AND NO JOKERS ARE PART OF THE HAND, A BONUS IS GIVEN: DOUBLE VALUE. EXCHANGED JOKERS FROM AN EXPOSURE CAN MAKE THE HAND JOKERLESS.

EXCEPTION: SINGLES & PAIRS GROUP—NO BONUS.

STANDARD BASED ON EIGHT FLOWERS AND EIGHT JOKERS

Run—means consecutive numbers. **Pair**-2 like tiles; **Pung**-3; **Kong**-4; **Quint**-5; **Sextet**-6. 1 color—any 1 suit; 2 colors-any 2 suits; 3 colors-3 suits. **F**-Flower; **X**-Exposed; **C**-Concealed; **D**-Dragon; **R**-Red D; **Wh**-White D; **G**-Green D. **Matching Dragons: Craks with Reds, Dots with Whites, Bams with Greens.**

Note: White Dragon is used also as ZERO "0". It can be USED with any suit (Craks, Bams or Dots).

ALL TILES FACED DOWN AND MIXED. EAST ROLLS DICE and total number thrown designates where East breaks wall. Each player picks 4 tiles for 3 rounds. East then picks next first and third top tiles and other players one tile each.

CHARLESTON (Flowers May Be Passed During Any Pass Including Courtesy But Jokers May Never Be Passed.)

First Charleston compulsory—three passes (right, across, left).

Second Charleston optional—three passes (left, across, right).

Blind pass of 1, 2, or 3 tiles permitted on last pass of either Charleston, without looking at them.

Courtesy pass-optional "0", 1, 2, or 3 tiles-with player opposite, whether one or two Charlestons are played.

Charleston is completed. East starts play by discarding 14th tile; players on the right of East pick and discard in rotation. Jokers may be discarded at any time during the game and named the same as previous discard. Jokers may be used to replace any tiles in any Pung, Kong, Quint or Sextet only. Joker or Jokers may be replaced in any exposure with like tile or tiles by any player, whether picked from wall or in player's hand, when it is player's turn. Joker or Jokers can **NEVER** be used for **single** tile, or for a **pair**.

1. NO PICKING OR LOOKING AHEAD.
2. When two players want the same discard, one player for an Exposure and another for Mah Jongg, Mah Jongg declarer always has preference.
3. When two players want the same tile for exposure, player next in turn to discarder has preference.
4. When two players want the same tile for Mah Jongg, player next in turn to discarder has preference.
5. A tile may not be claimed for Exposure or Mah Jongg after player next in turn has picked and racked or discarded a tile.

PLAYERS SHOULD NOT THROW IN HANDS UNTIL MAH JONGG IS VERIFIED.

MISCALLED TILE: A tile cannot be claimed until correctly named. Correctly named tile may then be called for an Exposure or Mah Jongg. HOWEVER, If Mah Jongg is called with the incorrectly named tile, the game ceases. Then, miscaller pays claimant four times the value of the hand. Others do not pay.

A hand is dead when it has too few or too many tiles during play or an incorrect number of exposed tiles. Dead hand ceases to pick and discard, pays winner same as other players.

At no time may a tile be called to complete a pair including flower for anything but Mah Jongg in an Exposed or Concealed Hand.

A discarded Flower may be claimed to complete the required number of Flowers for Mah Jongg in a Concealed Hand.

A discarded Flower may be claimed to complete Pung, Kong, Quint or Sextet of Flowers for Exposure or Mah Jongg in an exposed Hand.

Player is permitted to discard a Flower at any time during the game and call it "Flower".

RULES FOR BETTORS: Bettor pays or receives same as player bet on.

MAH JONGG IN ERROR

1. If a player declares Mah Jongg in error and does not expose the hand and all other hands are intact, play continues without penalty.

2. If a player declares Mah Jongg in error and exposes the hand and all other hands are intact, game continues but declarer's hand is dead. The same penalty applies for calling a discard and making an incorrect exposure. DEAD HAND DISCONTINUES PLAYING, DOES NOT PICK OR DISCARD. Pays winner full value of hand.

3. If a player declares Mah Jongg in error and one other player exposes part or all of the hand, the game continues with the two remaining players whose hands are intact. If more than one player, other than erring declarer, exposes part or all of the hand, game cannot continue. Erring declarer pays double the value of the incorrect hand to the one player whose hand is intact.

When writing for any information, please send a stamped self-addressed envelope to:

NATIONAL MAH JONGG LEAGUE, INC. 250 West 57th Street, New York, N.Y. 10107
(212) 246-3052 FAX (212) 246-4117 www.nationalmahjonggleague.org
Become a member: $7.00 includes Score Card & Bulletin

Printed in the USA

Tape this edge
to the other
red-starred
edge.

★ ★ ★

What Would You Do?

Here is a quiz whose answers focus on the issues we discussed. With generous permission from the National Mah Jongg League, the 2009 card is reproduced here to use as the card of reference to answer some of the questions below.

(My answers follow, but try not to peek. Good Luck!)

Here are some common situations that demand a decision. What would you do?

1. The game is in its early stages and you have a definite hand in mind which requires a Pung of 5Bams. You already have two 5Bams. Someone discards a 5Bam. Do you call it?

2. The game is in its late stages and you need a Kong of 8Bams. You have one 8Bam and two Jokers. One 8Bam has already been discarded and now a player discards the second 8Bam. Do you call it?

3. What Section and which hand are being pursued when the Exposures of a Kong of 4Craks and Kong of 5Dots have been made?

4. What tiles do you not discard?

5. Explain the concept of High vs. Low.

6. Your hand requires a Kong of Flowers. You have two and a Joker toward that combination. Two Flowers have already been discarded. A third is now discarded. Do you call it?

7. There is one Wall left plus three picks (12 tiles) from East's Wall. Someone exposes a Pung of 6Dots, using a Joker. Your hand requires a Pair of 6Dots. What do you do?

8. A player has exposed a Pung of 3Crak and then exposes a Pung of 9Dot. What do these Exposures reveal?

9. It's close to the end of the game, you have two picks left. You are "waiting" for Mah Jongg and other players are discarding Jokers. Your pick is a 7Bam, which you do not need. Do you discard it?

10. After the first Charleston, you end up with two very good possibilities for a hand. You have six tiles toward one hand and five tiles toward the other. What do you do?

11. An Exposure of a Pung of 8Craks is made. A second Exposure of a Kong of Red is exposed. What do you not discard?

12. What are the situations you would not exchange a tile for someone's exposed Joker?

13. What is the Number One critical criterion for choosing one hand over another?

14. What is racking? Why should you rack your tile?

15. A player discards a Joker. What is the message?

16. Explain a "safe" discard and a "hot" discard.

17. You are fairly sure you have the Mahj tile for an opponent's hand. The game is about ⅔ over. Do you discard it or not?

18. How many and which hand(s) are being pursued when Pungs of two different Dragons are exposed?

19. A Kong of 5Dots and a Kong of 7Dots are exposed. What is your conclusion about the hand and how do you defend against it?

20. A Pung of 9Crak is exposed. What is your conclusion about the hand being pursued?

21. From the tiles below, what Section(s)/hand(s) would you pursue?

   F 22 9, 1 3 7, 4 5 6, JJ, W.

22. Name three definite "No Nos" of the Charleston.

23. What are "maybe" tiles?

ANSWERS

1. No. **Wait** to either pick the tile, or a Joker or until the 4th 5Bam is discarded. Early disclosure helps your opponents.

2. Probably, depending on how close the end the game is and how close to Mah Jongg you are. If the game is about 3/4ths over and you are close to Mahj, (one or two tiles away), call. If it's almost over, (3 or 4 picks) there's little chance of winning and little advantage to call and your Exposure may be of great advantage to the other players.

3. The 5th hand in the Consecutive Run Section.

4. Later in the game, do not discard 3Bams, 6Bams, or Flowers. Early in the game, discard 3Bams, 6Bams, or Flowers.

5. High vs.Low relates to the odd Section. It refers to hands that require low numbers: 1,3,5, as opposed to high numbers: 5,7,9. If the odd-numbered tiles are predominately low, look for hands that require low numbers and if they are predominately high, look for hands that require high numbers.

6. If the game is about half over, probably, no. Flowers are being freely discarded. There are eight Flowers and five can be accounted for. There are still three more, so wait. You might pick one or a Joker. But, if the game is closer to the end, then call.

7. Your chances of picking the last 6Dot are very slim, but not impossible. And you might pick a Joker. If someone else picks the last 6Dot and exchanges the Joker for it, there is still about 50 tiles left in the Wall

from which you have about 10 or more chances to pick new tiles. So you still have a reasonable chance to be able to change your losing hand into a winning one.

8. The hand the player has exposed is 7th 369 hand and is Concealed. Call the player "Dead."

9. Most assuredly No. Even if you think the 7Bam is safe, you don't know how many Jokers an opponent has and is waiting for a 7Bam to complete the combination for Mah Jongg.

10. You have two options.
   You can stop the Charleston or abandon one hand.
   Check the card to see how many Pairs each hand requires. Choose the hand that requires no Pairs or the hand that requires the fewest number of Pairs. If you have the Pairs required for one hand but not the other, choose that hand and abandon the other.
   If both hands are equal, choose the hand that has six tiles over the hand that has five.

11. It's the 4th 2468 hand. Unless the game is in its early stages, (it's probably not, if two Exposures have been made) don't discard 2Craks or Flowers. If it's early, then discard 2Craks or Flowers.

12. Your exchange may give your opponent a Jokerless hand. If there is more than one Joker used in the Exposure, it's probably OK. But do not exchange a Joker for a tile unless it is to your advantage. If you are waiting for a tile to complete a Pair, you cannot use the Joker. Therefore, it is not to your advantage.

13. The critical factor is the number of Pairs each hand requires.

14. Racking is placing the picked Wall tile immediately into your rack next to the other tiles. It is a defensive strategy that denies the opportunity to any other player to call for the just discarded tile.

15. The player is most likely waiting for a tile to complete a Pair for Mah Jongg, and maybe going for a Joker-less hand or a Singles and Pairs hand.

16. A safe discard is a tile that another player does not or cannot call. Most discards are safe in the early stages of the game. A hot discard is a tile that has not been discarded during the game and usually occurs later in the game. Any tile, at the end of the game is potentially hot, except the Joker.

17. Usually No. It's too close to the end of the game and the chances of it being the opponent's Mahj tile is great. But if you are two tiles away or "waiting" for Mahj yourself, even though it's close to the end of the game, (there are still five or six picks left in the Wall) you might take a chance. If you are sure you have the Mahj tile, do not discard it and break up your hand.

18. Two, the 6th 369 hand and the 6th Winds/Dragons hand. The 6th Consecutive Run hand is Concealed.

19. The hand is the 3rd Consecutive Run hand. Early on, discard 6s. Later on, don't discard 6s. And keep track of how many 6s are already discarded. If, for example, three 6Bams are discarded, challenge and call the hand "Dead."

20. There are two Exposed hands that can use a Pung of nines: the 3rd Winds/Dragons hand and the 4th Consecutive Run hand. There are three other hands that can use a Pung of nines, all Concealed: the last 13579 hand, the last 369 hand and the last Consecutive Run hand. If any Exposure besides a Pung of eights is made, call the hand "Dead."

21. The Power is the Pair of 2s and the Jokers. The Sections that use 2s are the even and Consecutive Run.

F 22 46 JJ   7 even (reflects the 1st even hand.)

F 1 22 3 456 JJ 9 consecutive

Choose the 5th Consecutive Run hand, because even though both hands have seven tiles to begin, the consecutive hand requires one Pair over the even hand which requires three Pairs.

F 22 46 JJ(88) 7 tiles

F 22 3J 4J   7 tiles

22. Do not pass a Pair of anything.

Do not Pass Flowers.

Pass disparate tiles.

Do not pass more than two different Wind tiles.

Do not pass all tiles of the same Suit.

23. In the Charleston, "Maybe" tiles are tiles not closely connected to the Section you are pursuing, but kept as "maybe" useful later. Usually they are not.

Chinese Mah Jongg vs. American Mah Jongg

All the variations of Mah Jongg, including the American version, are direct descendants of the "parent" Chinese Mah Jongg. The "offspring," while retaining the core of the parent, not surprisingly, are all different. The question then is How does the American version differ from its parent? How is it the same?

American Mah Jongg is basically a simplified version of the Chinese game—still as challenging as the original. But in Chinese Mah Jongg, the goal is not just to win. In the Chinese game a winning hand is "scored," so the goal is to win with the highest scoring hand possible and to maximize its points.

A basic Chinese winning hand consists of any three Kongs and any Pair, called "Eyes." But it may also contain other combinations of any Pungs, Kongs, Pairs and/or Chows. Chows are runs of numbers in the same Suit—2,3,4, 5,6,7, etc.

The number of points a winning hand can score varies, according to who is the winner (East position gets bonus points for winning), what kind of tiles are used for a winning hand, Dragons, Winds, (called Honor tiles), all odd or even numbers, what combinations (Pungs, Kongs, all Pairs, Chows (worth fewer points than

Pungs or Kongs), one Suit (Clear Hand) vs. 2 or more Suits (Mixed Hand). Points are assigned for exposed (melds) vs. concealed combinations the winning hand contains, point values may be doubled or tripled. There are "Special" hands, and "Limit" hands that limit the points the hand is worth. The winner adds up all the points he/she can muster and then translates them into money per point, so a winner could potentially be a BIG winner if the hand scores lots of points.

Being an accountant is a good background to have to play Chinese Mah Jongg.

Another feature of the Chinese game is that the Flower tiles, called Bonus tiles, are worth extra points, if a player has one or picks one. But they are not included as part of the hand. There are eight of these Bonus tiles—divided into four "Flower" and four "Season" tiles. And there are no such things as Jokers or a "Charleston." Chinese mah jongg is played with 144 tiles and do not come with racks. The tiles stand upright in front of each player.

The biggest changes to American Mah Jongg occurred when the National Mah Jongg League created a "one size fits all" scoring system that set a specific "Value" for each hand and invented the "card," a unique idea, not found in other variations. It limited the number of hands that a player could play, not a rule in the Chinese game. The kinds of hands—Winds, Dragons, consecutive numbers, odd, even numbers, etc. were organized into distinct groups (sections) and the League ingeniously devised a logical and simple way to describe the specific combinations required for each hand within each group using color coding. The early Mah Jongg League's rules incorporated the eight bonus tiles as part of a hand. The designation of honor tiles was eliminated. And there are no Chows in American Mah Jongg. The first "League" sets came with upwards of 18 to 22 Flower tiles, some of which were used as "Joker." Gradually, Quint, Year hands, Singles and Pairs as well as "Equation" hands—addition and multiplication, appeared on the card and by the mid-1960s, the number of Flower and designated Joker tiles were fixed at eight each. Strangely, as it turns out, in simplifying the game, the American version is more restrictive than the original.

Although many of the Chinese game's rules and procedures have been modified or eliminated, we still retain much of the "parent" in the American game. The kinds of hands—odds, evens, Wind/Dragon hands, consecutive run, Like numbers—are all part of both games. The combinations of Pairs, Pungs, Kongs, one, two and three Suited hands again are in both versions. Building the "Wall"—seen as the Garden Wall, the City Wall, or the Great Wall of China, breaking the Wall, picking 13 tiles for the hand, retaining East as the designated "starter" with 14 tiles, the rules to "Call," the procedure to Expose, the direction of play from the right of East vs. new Walls from the left of East, and many more constraints, all stem from the original. And you still need 14 tiles to win.

So even though the two games are "different," they still are basically the same. Indeed, now you know why we play with eight Flower tiles and   four of them are sometimes designated with the Seasons.

✥ APPENDIX 2 ✥

The Genesis of American Mah Jongg

In the decades following World War I, American society underwent revolutionary changes, economic, political and societal. The stock market exploded upward, the Middle-Class emerged, women got the vote (1920), Prohibition was passed (1922) and then repealed (1933), the Great Depression infected the country and the New Deal was its antidote. The Flapper smoked cigarettes in public, cut her hair, hiked her skirts, and showed a bare back. Jazz and the Charleston were born and Americans became obsessed by the Far East—the exotic, mysterious, hidden distant. Food, art, fashion, and literature reflected the fascination for all things "Oriental." And nothing represented the exotic East more than the Chinese game, Mah Jongg. Ads for free classes, books, magazines, newspaper articles, clubs, sets, clothes, objects d'art, tchokes flooded the market—all about Mah Jongg—how to play it, how to dress for it, how to plan the food for your Mah Jongg party. Mah Jongg hit Broadway in 1924 with a song by Eddie Cantor called When Ma is Playing Mah Jongg in a play called Kid Boots, directed by the "Great Ziegfeld." By the 1930s every department store worth its salt, had counters overflowing with Mah Jongg sets, displayed at the front of the store so that when a shopper entered, they would be the first thing seen, and, hopefully, purchased. There was even a TV program in the '50s that taught the fundamentals of the game. Mah Jongg players were modern, hip, intellectually superior, and its popularity was legendary.

As an example of the status of players of the game, in 1923, the Boston Transcript of May 29th, devoted an entire page to the subject of Mah Jongg and "among the notables credited with being devotees were the late Pres. Harding, ... Justices of the Supreme Court, members of the Cabinet and their families."

As with the general ignorance of China and the East, so the game of Mah Jongg was cloaked in myth and lore almost since its introduction to the United States in 1920 by Joseph Babcock. Mr. Babcock was an "oil man," employed by Standard Oil in China early in the Century. Based in Shanghai and as a friend of the British establishment, he was introduced to the game being played in their "clubs." And being a man of vision and entrepreneurial spirit, he saw the possibilities of turning the popular success of the Chinese game into an equally popular and profitable success in America. So upon his return to the States in 1920, fearing the American public would not take to the Chinese version of the game, he proceeded to produce a simplified version of the game he played in China. He imported an "Anglicized" version of sets by putting numerals on the Suit tiles and writing a booklet called "Babcock's Rules for Mah Jongg," which was included as a learning tool with the sets.

At first, the game was only a moderate success, but it quickly became the focus of marketing hype. In A.D. Millington's book, The Complete Book of Mah-Jongg, the Chapter on the "History of Mah-Jongg" tells us that the "dubious legends, ill-founded speculations, improbable myths... not to mention deliberate falsification and fabrication" abounded. He attributes these practices to the importers and retailers of the sets "who were by no means so scrupulous as to think it necessary to confine themselves to facts in their promotional literature," claiming "an exalted history of hundreds... thousands of years" and perhaps "invented or played by Confucius," probably the only Chinese name known to Americans.

Perhaps the reader will be surprised that what follows was believed and expounded as the "true" beginnings of the game by reputable writers. Here's one example.

A book written by R.J.F. Gerstle in 1922 titled, Mah Jong, The Green Book (the cover was green) begins his

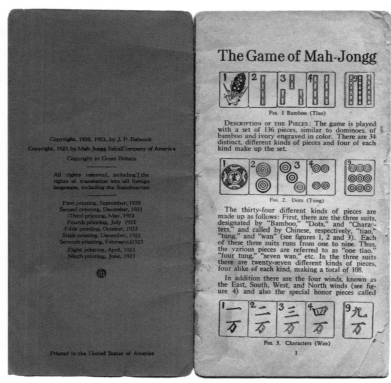

Babcock's Rules.

81

preface by stating that "…the author is able to present to his readers… the most authentic and recognized story of the game…" He credits the editor of the China Weekly Review as his authority. He asserts the true beginning of the game was devised by a fisherman named Sze, as a way to keep his crew from thinking about and thereby becoming sea-sick by providing them with a game that was so fascinating they became completely absorbed in it, and soon forgot about becoming sea-sick. He unequivocally states, "So there you have the origin of Ma-Jongg…"

Milton C. Work was a gentleman who was the Editor of "Auction Bridge and Mah Jongg Magazine," a separate Mah Jongg Department of the N.Y. Herald Tribune. In 1924 he published a book called Mah-Jongg Up-To-Date. (Price: $1.00.) In the introduction he writes, "Concerning the birth of this game, we have been favored with many theories." Among them "legends which tell us that Chinese royalty…played in secret…keeping all knowledge…from the common people," "a Chinese General…invented the game to amuse his soldiers during a long drawn-out siege," as well as the tale of fisherman Sze. He then goes on to assert that people of "practical temperament" will be "content with the established fact that this tile game has been popular in China for at least four decades…." which places the appearance of Mah Jongg around 1880. That date is confirmed by the first references to the game in the Chinese literature and the appearance of mah jongg sets—one exhibited at the Columbia Exhibition in 1893 and one brought from China by the American Consul at Foochow and given to the Long Island Historical Society. Both are described in the Annual Report of 1893 of the United States National Museum.

As confusion dominated the origins of the game, so confusion dominated the playing of the game. In Chinese Mah Jongg the goal of the game is to win with a hand that scores high point values—translated into money for the winner. The higher the point value, the higher the monetary value. Because the scoring systems were complicated, confusing and frequently controversial, they became the focus of disagreement and heated argument among the early players. The resulting chaos led to the glut of books, newspaper comments and magazine articles, all written by mah jongg "authorities," describing the "one and only" correct method of playing and scoring.

Mr. Work's book, referenced above, was sub-titled the "Latest Word on Mah Jongg" and, contained the

How to stay cool in 1924.

"New Official Laws of Mah-Jongg"—all 100 of them, compiled from a "survey" of Mah Jongg players and their preferred method of playing. The cover of his book reads "These Laws... are the American Laws of Mah Jongg which will be universally used, having been standardized under the direction of the recognized experts, JOSEPH P. BABCOCK, R.F. FOSTER, LEE F. HARTMAN, JOHN H. SMITH AND MILTON C. WORK." Unfortunately, not many players read his book nor paid attention to the "Laws." Dissention and disagreement reigned. By the early 1930s the game, played predominately by men, lost most of its appeal.

A game from the era of America's first mah jongg craze.

But not to women, who, being mostly home-makers and stay-at-home moms, were delighted to have a new, stimulating, social activity to fill hours of new and liberating leisure time.

In 1937, the National Mah Jongg League made its official appearance. Because there still were no standard rules, its purpose was to bring order out of chaos. Four women emerged as the moving force: Viola Cecil, Dorothy Myerson, Herma Jacobs, and Hortense Potter. In 1938 Mrs. Cecil published a book titled, MAHJ: The American Version of an Ancient Game. The title of Mrs. Cecil's book refers to the Confucius tale, which only added authenticity to its claim as the origin of Mah Jongg. That myth still persists today.

Her book retained many aspects of the original Chinese Mah Jong game, but settled the controversial scoring by giving each hand a definite value and produced a "card" that proscribed hands a player could play, making the game much simpler. According to the archives of the League, the first cards were mimeographed and sold for 10 cents each to about 100 players.

And the rest, as we say, is history. The game, played in 1937, is basically the same as the one we play today. There have been some changes to the game—evolving changes to the card and, in the 60's, the fixing of the number of Flower tiles and Joker tiles at eight. Today, the game's popularity is again legendary, with League membership of about 300,000—and they all follow the same rules!

The Evolution of the Card

These cards from past years demonstrate interesting ways the game of American mah jongg has evolved while retaining the same core rules.

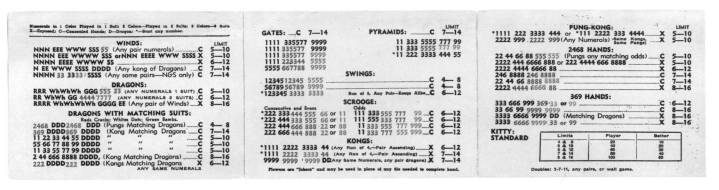

Numerals in 1 Color Played in 1 Suit; 2 Colors—Played in 2 Suits; 3 Colors—3 Suits
X—Exposed; C—Concealed Hands; D—Dragon; *—Start any number.

WINDS: LIMIT
NNN EEE WWW SSS 55 (Any pair numerals) C   5—10
NNNN EEE WWWW SSS or NNN EEEE WWW SSSS X   5—10
NNNN EEEE WWWW SS C   6—12
N EE WWW SSSS DDDD (Any kong of Dragons) C   7—14
NNNN 33 3333 SSSS (Any same pairs—N&S only) C   7—14

DRAGONS:
RRR WhWhWh GGG 555 33 (ANY NUMERALS 1 SUIT) .C   5—10
RR WhWh GG 4444 7777 (ANY NUMERALS 2 SUITS) .C   6—12
RRRR WhWhWhWh GGGG EE (Any pair of Winds) X   8—16

DRAGONS WITH MATCHING SUITS:
Reds Cracks; Whites Dots; Green Bambs.
2468 DDD 2468 DDD (Pungs Matching Dragons) C   4— 8
369 DDDD 369 DDDD (Kong Matching Dragons) C   7—14
11 22 33 44 55 DDDD   "   "   " C   5—10
55 66 77 88 99 DDDD   "   "   " C   5—10
11 33 55 77 99 DDDD   "   "   " C   5—10
2 44 666 8888 DDDD   " (Kong Matching Dragons) .C   8—16
222 DDDD 222 DDDD (Kongs Matching Dragons   X   6—12
                              ANY SAME NUMERALS

GATES: ...C   7—14
1111 335577 9999
1111 335577 9999
1111 335577 9999
1111 223344 5555
5555 667788 9999

PYRAMIDS: C   7—14   LIMIT
            11 333 5555 777 99
            11 333 5555 777 99
*11 222 3333 444 55

SWINGS:
1234512345 5555 C   4— 8
56789 56789 9999 C   4— 8
*123345 3333 3333   Run of 5, Any Pair—Kongs Alike ..C   6—12

SCROOGE:
Consecutive and Evens   Odds
*222 333 444 555 66 or 11   111 333 555 777   99 ...C   6—12
*222 444 333 555 66 or 11   111 555 333 777   99 ...C   6—12
222 444 666 888 22 or 88   11 333 555 777 999 ..C   6—12
222 666 444 888 22 or 88   11 333 777 555 999 .C   6—12

KONGS:
*1111 2222 3333 44 (Any Run of 4,—Pair Ascending) ...X   6—12
*1111 2222 3333 44 (Any Run of 4,—Pair Ascending) ...X   7—14
9999 9999 9999 DD (Any Same Numerals, any pair dragons) X   7—14

Flowers are "Jokers" and may be used in place of any tile needed to complete hand.

PUNG-KONG:
*1111 222 3333 444 or *111 2222 333 4444   X   5—10
2222 999 2222 999 (Any Numerals) Same Kongs, X   5—10
                                Same Pungs
2468 HANDS:
22 44 66 88 555 555 (Pungs any matching odds) ...C   5—10
2222 444 6666 888 or 222 4444 666 8888 X   5—10
2222 4444 6666 88 X   6—12
246 8888 246 8888 C   7—14
22 44 66 8888 8888 C   7—14
2222 4444 6666 88 X   8—16

369 HANDS:
333 666 999 369 33 or 99 C   6—12
33 66 99 9999 9999 C   8—16
3333 6666 9999 DD (Matching Dragons) X   8—16
3333 6666 9999 33 or 99 X   8—16

KITTY:
STANDARD

Limits	Player	Better
4 & 8	20	10
5 & 10	40	20
6 & 12	60	30
7 & 14	80	40
8 & 16	100	80

Doubles: 3-7-11, any pairs, or wall game.

Note: Flowers are Jokers.

		BOUQUET HANDS—CONCEALED	Non E.	East
2 Flowers	FF	1955 · 1955 · 1955	c140-280	
2 "	FF	22 4 6 88 22 4 6 88	c120-240	
2 "	FF	369D 369D 369D	c120-240	
2 "	FF	13579 2468 369	c120-240	
3 "	FFF	11 2345678 99	c120-240	
3 "	FFF	12234 222 222 (Any Run 4 Nos. Pair & Pungs to Match)	c140-280	
3 "	FFF	33 66 99 369 66 (Pair 3, 6 or 9 in 3rd Suit)	c120-240	
3 "	FFF	NN EE WW SS R.Wh G	c120-240	
4 "	†FFFF	22 44 66 88 DD	c120-240	
4 "	FFFF	11 33 55 77 99	c120-240	
4 "	FFFF	11 22 33 44 55 (Any Run 5 Nos. Pairs)	c120-240	
4 "	FFFF	RR WhWh GG N E W S	c120-240	
5 "	FFFFF	111 555 888 (Pungs any Nos.)	c120-240	
		BOUQUET HAND—EXPOSED		
2 "	FF	1111 4444 EEEE (3 Kongs of Anything. Any Suits, Winds or Dragons)	x150-300	
		NO FLOWER HANDS		
No Flowers		NN EE WW SS RR WhWh GG	c150-300	
"		11 22 33 44 55 66 77 (Any Run 7 Nos. Pairs)	c150-300	

Do NOT play with more than 22 Flowers. Do NOT start with any Free Flowers on rack.
For reference on Bouquet Hands, Concealed or Exposed, see Rules 10, 11A, 11B.

Note: Do not play with more than 22 Flowers.

			Non E.	East
Dragons	RRRRR WhWhWhWh GGGGG	(Kong Wh.)	x100	-200
	RRRRR WhWh GGGGGG	(Pair Wh.)	x120	-240

[Pair and Kong can only be called for Mah Jongg, not for exposure. Flowers may also replace Whites.]

SEPTETTES

			Non E.	East
Winds	NNNNNNN SSSSSSS	(This way only)	x100	-200
	EEEEEEE WWWWWWW	(This way only)	x100	-200
	NNNNNNN DDDDDDD	(Any W. Any D.)	x100	-200
3-6-9	†3333333 DDDDDDD	(Nos. 3, 6 or 9—matching D.)	x100	-200
	3333333 6666666		x 90	-180
	3333333 6666666		x 90	-180
	6666666 9999999		x 90	-180
	6666666 9999999		x 90	-180
1's & 9's	1111111 9999999		x 90	-180
	1111111 9999999		x 90	-180
2's & 8's	2222222 8888888		x 90	-180
	2222222 8888888		x 90	-180

FLOWER HAND (Unlimited Flowers)

			Non E.	East
	FFFFFFF 4444444	(Sept. of Flowers & Sept. of Anything.)	x140	-280

[A discarded Flower may only be claimed to complete Septette of Flowers for Exposure or to complete a Septette of Flowers for Mah Jongg.]

			Non E.	East
Same No.	1111111 1111111	(Any Same Nos.)	x	90-180
Consecutives	1111111 2222222	(Run any 2 consecutive Nos.)	x	90-180
	1111111 2222222	(Run any 2 consecutive Nos.)	x	90-180
Odds	1111111 3333333		x	90-180
	1111111 3333333		x	90-180
	3333333 5555555		x	90-180
	3333333 5555555		x	90-180
	5555555 7777777		x	90-180
	5555555 7777777		x	90-180
	7777777 9999999		x	90-180
	7777777 9999999		x	90-180
Evens	2222222 4444444		x	90-180
	2222222 4444444		x	90-180
	4444444 6666666		x	90-180
	4444444 6666666		x	90-180
	6666666 8888888		x	90-180
	6666666 8888888		x	90-180

1 color–1 suit; 2 colors–2 suits; 3 colors–3 suits. F–Flowers; X–Exposed; C–Concealed.
†Matching Dragons: Cracks with Reds, Dots with Whites, Bambs with Greens. D–Dragons; R–Red D; Wh.–White D; G–Green D.

FLOWERS	13579 (Continued)	Non E. East
0	**11 33 55 77 99 DDDD** (Matching Dragons)	**c160-320**
0	**111 333 555 777 99** or 111 333 555 777 99	**x150-300**
0	**11 333 5555 777 99** or 11 333 5555 **777 99**	**c170-340**
	2468	
3	**FFF** 22 4 6 8 **222 222** (Any Pair 2, 4, 6, 8 and Matching Pungs)	**c150-300**
2	**FF 222 444 666 888** or 222 444 666 888	**x140-280**
0	2 44 66 8 2 44 66 8 **22** or **88**	**c140-280**
0	22 44 22 44 66 **8888**	**c160-320**
2	**FF 22 44 66 88 DDDD** (Matching Dragons)	**c160-320**
0	2222 4444 6666 88	**x170-340**
0	2222 4444 6666 88 (Pair of 8's to Match 4's)	**x170-340**
	369	
2	**FF 33 66 99 RR WhWh GG** (3 Suits)	**c150-300**
2	**FF 333 666 999 DDD** (Dragons Matching 6's)	**x160-320**
2	**FF 3 66 999 3 66 999** (This Way Only)	**c160-320**
4	**FFFF** 33 6 9 **333 333** (Any Pair 3, 6, 9 and Matching Pungs)	**c150-300**
0	336 33 66 9 **33 66 99**	**c160-320**
2	**FF 3333 6666 9999** or 3333 6666 **9999**	**x160-320**
0	33 666 33 666 **9999** (This Way Only)	**c170-340**

FLOWERS	ANY LIKE NUMERALS	Non E. East
5	**FFFFF** 888 888 888 (Pungs Any Like No.)	**c170-340**
2	**FF** 111 DDD 111 DDD (Any Like Nos. Matching Dragons)	**x140-280**
0	111 DDDD 111 DDDD or 1111 DDD 1111 DDD (Any Like No. Match. Drags.)	**x170-340**
0	1118888 111 8888 or 1111 888 1111 888 (Any 2 Like Nos.)	**x160-320**
	SEVEN HANDS (These Nos. Only)	
2	**FF 1111+6666=7777** or 1111+6666=7777	**x170-340**
2	**FF 2222+5555=7777** or 2222+5555=7777	**x170-340**
2	**FF 3333+4444=7777** or 3333+4444=7777	**x170-340**
	ADDITION HANDS (These Nos. Only)	
4	**FFFF 5555+6666=11** or 5555+6666=11	**x160-320**
4	**FFFF 6666+7777=13** or 6666+7777=13	**x160-320**
4	**FFFF 7777+8888=15** or 7777+8888=15	**x160-320**
4	**FFFF 8888+9999=17** or 8888+9999=17	**x160-320**
	WINDS AND DRAGONS	
2	**FF NNN SSS 11 11 11** (Any Pairs of Like Odds)	**c150-300**
2	**FF EEE WWW 22 22 22** (Any Pairs of Like Evens)	**c150-300**
0	NNN 1111 SSS 1111 or **NNNN 111 SSSS 111** (Any Like Odds)	**x160-320**
0	EEE 2222 WWW 2222 or **EEEE 222 WWWW 222** (Any Like Evens)	**x160-320**
2	**FF NN EE WW SS DDDD** (Any Kong of Dragons)	**c150-300**
2	**FF RRRR WhWhWhWh GGGG**	**x170-340**
0	**NNN EEEE WWWW SSS** or **NNNN EEE WWW SSSS**	**x170-340**

These older cards have subtle (and not so subtle) changes in rules and hands.

STANDARD BASED ON 12 FLOWERS PLUS FOUR BIG JOKERS. BIG JOKERS MAY BE USEI TO REPLACE ANY TILES IN ANY HAND. See Additional Use of Big Jokers on Face of Card

READ ALL RULES CAREFULLY

Run—means consecutive numbers. **Pair**—2 like tiles; **Pung**—3; **Kong**—4; **Quint**—5; **Sextette**—(**1 color**—any 1 suit; **2 colors**—any 2 suits; **3 colors**—3 suits. **F**—Flower; **X**—Exposed; **C**—Concealed **D**—Dragon; **R**—Red D; **Wh.**—White D; **G**—Green D.

Matching Dragons: Cracks with Reds, Dots with Whites, Bambs with Greens.

ALL TILES FACED DOWN AND MIXED. EAST ROLLS DICE. The total number thrown designates wher East breaks wall. Each player picks 4 tiles for 3 rounds. East then picks next first and third top tile and other players one tile each. East starts play by discarding 14th tile; players to right of Eas pick and discard in rotation.

1. NO PICKING OR LOOKING AHEAD. 2. A hand is dead when it has too few or too many tiles durin play or an incorrect number of exposed tiles. Dead hand ceases to pick and discard, pays sam as other players.

CLAIMING DISCARDS

3.a When two players want the same discard, one player for an Exposure and another for Mah Jong Mah Jongg declarer always has preference. b. When two players want the same tile for Exposur or for Mah Jongg, player next in turn to discarder has preference. c. When two of same tile ar discarded in rapid succession, second must be taken.

4. A tile may not be claimed for Exposure or Mah Jongg after player next in turn has discarded c declared "Mah Jongg".

5.a Player is permitted to discard a Flower at any time during the game and call it "FLOWER" b. BIG JOKER may be discarded at any time during the game and called the same as th previous discard.

6.a Two like tiles in hand before third may be claimed for Pung in Exposed Hands.

 b Three like tiles in hand before fourth may be claimed for Kong in Exposed Hands.

 c A Flower cannot be used in any hand to replace the required pattern of any Numerals, Winds (Dragons, but the BIG JOKER may be used.

7. At no time may a tile be called to complete a pair including Flower, for anything but Mah Jong in an Exposed or Concealed Hand.

8a. A discarded Flower may be claimed to complete the Kong or Sextette of Flowers for Exposure (Mah Jongg in an Exposed Hand.

b A discarded Flower may be claimed to complete the required number of Flowers for Mah Jongg in a Concealed Hand.

c BIG JOKERS may replace any tiles in any hand, for anything.

MISCALLING

9.a A tile cannot be claimed until correctly named. Correctly named tile may then be called for an Exposure or Mah Jongg. No penalty.

b If incorrectly named tile is called for Mah Jongg, game ceases. Miscaller pays claimant twice the value of the hand. Other players do not pay.

MAH JONGG IN ERROR

10.a If a player declares Mah Jongg in error and does not expose the hand and all other hands are intact, play continues without penalty.

b If a player declares Mah Jongg in error and exposes part or all of the hand and all other hands are intact, play proceeds but declarer's hand is dead. DEAD HAND DISCONTINUES PLAYING, DOES NOT PICK OR DISCARD. Pays winner same as other players, double if East.

c If a player declares Mah Jongg in error (exposing or not exposing) and more than one player throws in or exposes their hands, the play cannot continue. Erring declarer pays one-half the value of the incorrect hand to the player whose hand is intact. East pays or receives double that amount.

RULES FOR BETTORS

1. Bets must not be disclosed or changed. At no time during the game may the bettor give any information until Mah Jongg is declared. Penalty: bet cancelled.

2. Bettor pays or receives full value of the hand.

3. Bettor pays or receives same penalty as player bet on. (Rule 9b—10b—10c)

CHARLESTON (Flowers May Be Passed During Any Pass Including Courtesy)

First Charleston compulsory—three passes (right, across, left).

Second Charleston optional—three passes (left, across, right).

Blind pass of 1, 2 or 3 tiles permitted on last pass of either Charleston.

Courtesy pass—optional 1, 2 or 3 tiles—with player opposite, whether one or two Charlestons are played.

When writing for any information, please send a stamped, self-addressed envelope to PRINTED IN U.S.A.

NATIONAL MAH JONGG LEAGUE, Inc., 250 W. 57th St., New York 19, N. Y.

Circle 6-3052   Membership 60¢ per year   Copyright 1963, U. S. and Canada

Some interesting differences are on the back of the card.

The Symbolism of Chinese Mah Jongg

When the Mah Jongg craze hit the American scene, the attraction to the game was encouraged, in no small measure, by a rampant and blatant blitz of commercialism. It was marketed as a social event, a time for friends and family parties, for fun and enjoyment. But in China, where the game was (and is) the "national pastime," Mah Jongg was serious business.

Chinese Mah Jongg emerges from a gradual evolution of many different card and tile games—invented, played and changed over time. Most of these games metaphorically incorporated aspects of the ancient Chinese philosophical tradition—the I Ching, or The Book of Changes.

The I Ching is a collection of "divine" formulas to resolve the questions of right and wrong behaviors, arrived at by "the casting of lots"—Luck, (which is probably why gambling is so popular in China) and the relationship between cause and effect—Skill. Let's then see how this game of Mah Jongg, retaining these roots, is a symbolic representation of the Universe, as described in the I Ching.

According to the I Ching, the origin of the Universe is T'ai-Chi, the Super Extreme—the Absolute. T'ai-Chi generates two modes or energies, the Yin and the Yang and from the pairing of these two, emerges Heaven and Earth. From Heaven and Earth, comes Man and all human events—past, present, and future and All Things Possible. Here then, is the hierarchy; after the Super Extreme, comes the three elements, Heaven, Earth, and Man, called The Three Extremes.

So how does Mah Jongg embody these three principles?

The Three Extremes are reflected in the tiles, primarily the Dragons. The White Dragon, called Po, we call "Soap", is blank or (mostly) white, denoting the Sky or Heaven. The Green Dragon, called Fa, means prosperity or flourishing, signifying the Earth and Nature. And the Red Dragon is called Chung, which means the middle or center, which is the element between Heaven and Earth—Man.

The colors of the Dragons are of also of significance—white denotes purity or Heaven, green is the color of the Earth and red is blood, the color of Life or Man.

And all the other tiles are related to these Three Extremes. The four Seasons, (stamped on the Flowers) denoting time, are a manifestation of Heaven's cycle—Spring, Summer, Autumn, and Winter. The four Winds represent space or regions of the Earth—North, East, South, and West. And the four Flowers, plum, orchid, chrysanthemum, and bamboo, reflect Life or Man.

What about the three Suits, called the Three Categories or variables? They are representative of movements of the Three Extremes. The Circles (Dots), called T'ung means "wheels," and represent the Wheels of Heaven, which now has come to represent cash or coins—business, wealth, commerce.

The Bamboo (Bams), called Chou, denotes the Axis of the Earth, or literally, long, thin, strong strands, not unlike the long, thin, strong strands of bamboo, now commonly interpreted to mean strength, service.

And the Character (Craks), called Shu, meaning "numbers," signifies the infinite changes and events in the Life of Man and now is used to signify the "myriad" or in Chinese, "Wan." In American Mah Jongg the Crak Suit is still referred to as the "Character" Suit.

A guiding principle of the I Ching tradition is the search for balance or Harmony out of the chaos of the Three Extremes, this being the obstacle and the goal of Life.

So when a player picks tiles from the Wall, it's the "casting of lots"—Luck. And when a player manipulates, changes, keeps or rejects, and strategizes the tiles, it's the relationship of cause and effect—Skill. Finally, when a player brings to fruition and completes a Mah Jongg hand, it is the Harmony that comes out of the chaos of indiscriminate tiles—The Three Extremes of Heaven, Earth and Man—thereby overcoming the obstacles and reaching the ultimate goal and fulfilling the idea.

And you thought you were just playing Mah Jongg!